HEY, WHY'D THE AUTHOR PUT THE UPSIDE-DOWN WRITING ON THE COVER??

Well, first off, he's a bit peculiar. Second, he likes to call himself an "author" even though he can't hardly write. And third, he thinks that most guidebooks suck—too boring and dry. So, he figured that some ... illiant multi-book buyer— ... , photoriffic, irreverend, ... s! But first, open this book ... 't like. Go find some new ... guidebook@yahoo.com

CURIOUS GORGE

A GUIDE BY SCOTT COOK

"Come visit us again and again. This is a state of excitement. But for heaven's sake, don't come here to live."

— Gov. Tom McCall, 1971

All exploration, text, and photography
Scott Cook

Design, layout, and editing
Moria Reynolds

2nd edition design and printing by Jody Conners, Ron Wells and Gary Asher of Maverick Publications, Bend OR

Back cover map courtesy of
Columbia River Gorge Commission

Curious Gorge
PO Box 861
Hood River, OR 97031
email: curiousgorgeguidebook@yahoo.com

Cover Photo: Gorge from hillside above Catherine Creek
Top Inset: Punchbowl Falls, Eagle Creek trail
2nd Inset: Mt. Hood from Panorama Point
3rd Inset: Cabin Creek Falls, Starvation Falls trail
Bottom Inset: Roadsde sign, Hwy 35, Hamlet of Mt. Hood

*Don't Panic – A tribute to the late Douglas Adams for writing the funniest Hitchhiker's Guide the galaxy has ever seen!

Warning: Hiking in the Columbia River Gorge can be dangerous. All the information in this book has been personally checked by the author to be accurate. Trail conditions do change though- trees fall, land slides, signs disappear, fees change. The author can accept no responsibility for any inconvenience, injury, or pregnancy due to the use of this guide.

DEDICATION

This guide is dedicated to **Nancy Russell**, founder of "Friends of the Columbia Gorge".

Nancy is a rare person. Her passion for the Gorge's splendor combined with her charismatic persuasiveness have yielded a tremendous legacy. The Gorge, as we see it today, would undoubtedly look much worse were it not for Nancy's heroic efforts to preserve and enhance the landscape. Nancy seeks results, not fame…shies from political limelight, instead enjoying personal delight in such pleasures as a wildflower-spangled hillside.

Many Gorge residents are unaware of Nancy's efforts on behalf of the Gorge (the author was completely unaware at the time of his first 2002 printing). In 1980 Nancy spearheaded the drive to protect the Gorge's scenic wonders, as well as its economic vitality, under the auspices of the first-of-its-kind "National Scenic Area". She founded the conservation group "Friends of the Gorge", first in order to get the Scenic Act passed in Congress, and subsequently to protect the Gorge from encroaching development while promoting recreational enhancement – more parks, more trails, more access!

If you are a person who treasures the beautiful Gorge scenery we see today, then you probably owe Nancy Russell a debt of gratitude. Without Nancy Russell and the Scenic Act, that gorgeous hillside over yonder, that thousand-foot bluff, that beautiful river canyon…they might have all been dotted with trophy homes, clear cuts, or developed into a casino or resort or something.

Thank you, Nancy. May future generations sing your praise as they discover the Gorge's wonders for themselves and learn of the visionaries who had the passion and wisdom to preserve it for them.

(Original) DEDICATION

"The beauties of the Gorge of the Columbia can never be forgotten by any visitor." *Samuel Lancaster*

I would like to thank the friends that have helped me explore and expand my love for the Columbia River Gorge: Kimberly Smith, Lisa Merkin, Rob McCready, Pam Davis, Brad Whiting, Christina Sproule, Mike Guernsey, Jeanette Burkhardt, Sky Robbins, Brad Cross, and many more.

A special thank you goes to Moria Reynolds. Without her these pageswould probably still be scribbled on napkins and receipts!

And finally, Mother Nature- thanks for 20 million years of Gorge-ous cataclysms. We all appreciate it!

Rock 'n' Roll Fame for Punchbowl Falls
(on the Eagle Creek Trail—entry #8)

The back cover of Styx's 1973 second album.
(Stop at Dog River Coffee in Hood River to see the original album up on the wall.)

Circa 1999 before the log fell down (see page 33)

AUTHOR'S NOTE

In the first edition (2002) of *Curious Gorge* I didn't include any info about myself. I didn't think people would care who wrote the book, but just whether the book was any good. I was wrong. People seem to be curious about what kind of person writes a guidebook like this one...so here goes...

I'm 40 years old, single, and have been living in Hood River since about 1995. Born in Chicago, went to college at Vanderbilt U. in Tennessee, majored in math and psychology. I have no formal training in either writing or photography.

I moved to Hood River pretty much just to windsurf, but once I got to the Gorge I became enraptured with the beauty and the amazing variety of activities. The magnificence of the Gorge inspired me to try to take photos—inspired me to learn those sneaky techniques to blur waterfalls, increase depth-of-field, use polarized filters...all that stuff.

The more of the Gorge that I discovered, the more addicted to discovery I became. I read every guidebook I could—hiking, waterfalls, flowers, geology, history, Gorge Guides, whatever! The more that I learned about this phenomenal Gorge, the more I realized that there was no single guidebook that does justice to the Gorge's variety of wonders. *Curious Gorge* was born...in my mind. But how to make a guidebook? I had no idea. I looked closely at all the ones I owned and decided on three principles: more photos, precise directions and drivetimes, and real-life language. I wanted to make a guidebook that honored the Gorge, was fun to use, and was also exact—no getting lost! Met Moria Reynolds and we spent three months merging her Pagemaker skills with my scattered ideas. We really didn't know what we were doing, but *Curious Gorge* finally got done.

Now, four years later, I've decided to try to "improve" it. So here's the new edition. Roughly half the photos are new (possibly better), there are seven new entries, and I deleted some lame entries. I tweaked my writing, the cover, and the map...and here it is. Hope you enjoy it—hope it inspires you to further explore our Gorge-ous slice of heaven. Hope it inspires you to help protect this national treasure.

From the original AUTHOR'S NOTE (2002)

...For 100 years people have popularized and touted the beauty of the Gorge; Sam Hill, Samuel Lancaster, Woody Guthrie, Governor Tom McCall, and Senator Mark Hatfield to name a few. The question remains: Do you popularize the Gorge in order to preserve it or do you keep it 'secret' to keep the masses away? Who is John Galt?

The Curious Gorge is not meant to increase tourism in the Gorge. That's the Tourism Bureau's job. My goal is to strengthen a visitor's or resident's appreciation of the uniqueness here. Certainly nobody wants the crowds of Yosemite or Yellowstone in Hood River. To this end, this guidebook will not be sold outside of the Gorge. It is only available from Portland to The Dalles. No website, no amazon, no Seattle, no San Francisco, nor Salt Lake City. You must already be here to get a copy.

Yes, my aim is to profit from this book, but not at the expense of the community and beauty that I love. My wish is that *The Curious Gorge* inspires people to partake of the Gorge's variety and expand their appreciation. Hopefully, increased appreciation and passion for the Gorge will, in some small way, help preserve the qualities that make this area so special—the people, beauty, sports, and history.

The Columbia River Gorge is worth protecting.
The Gorge needs friends, not just acquaintances.

Table of Contents

THE COLUMBIA GORGE.......
A WORK OF ART TO BE GIVEN THE
DEVOTION OF A LIFETIME

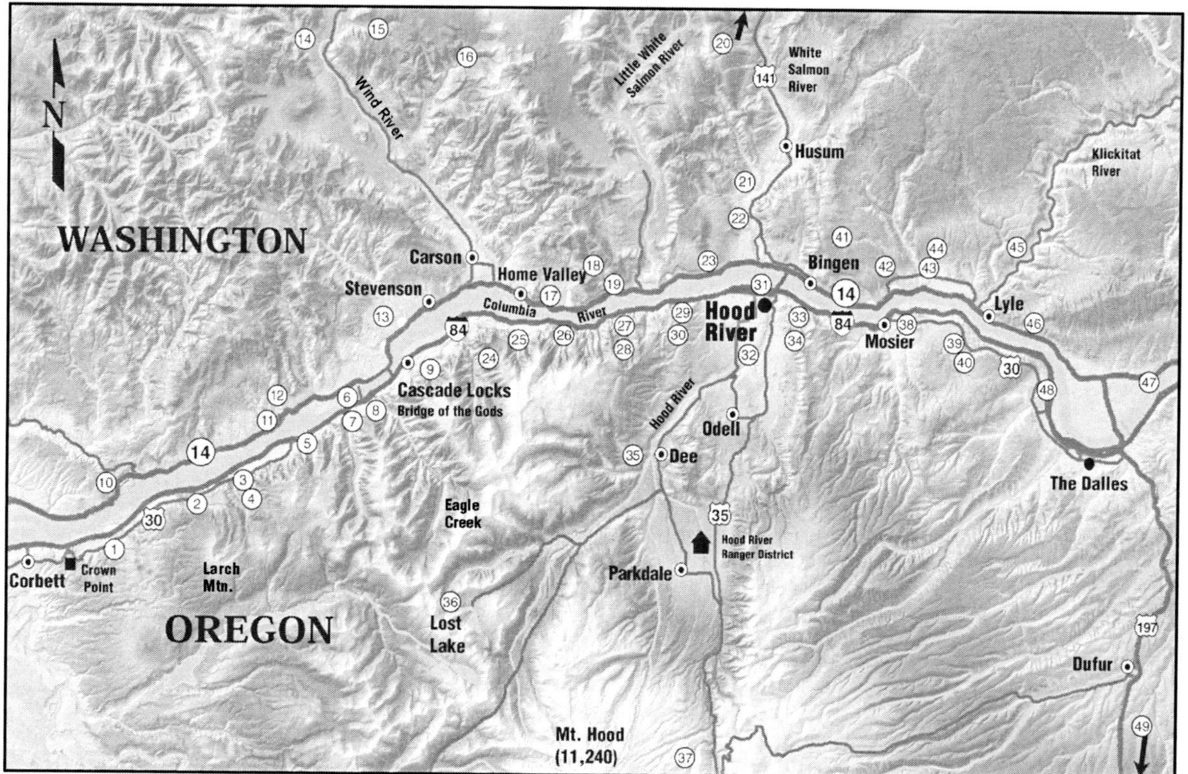

THE ROUNDTRIP TIME-GUESS:

These time guesses are an attempt to estimate a real-world time for each outing. Each one contains the "to" and "from" drivetimes from either Hood River or Portland, as well as an estimated time to actually do the hike or excursion. **These guesses are not the minimum time required!** These guesses include an estimate of time hanging-out, eating, photographing... or just reveling in the Gorge's glory. Some people might hurry and "beat" these guesses in their mad rush to do-more, do-more... but if they do they'll miss out, they'll be sorry...haste makes waste...and they'll probably be condemned to eternal damnation in the fiery pits of California!

Here's how a timeguess is figured—Use the quadratic equation:

$$x = \frac{-b \pm \sqrt{b^2 - 4ac}}{2a}$$

No, really, for example take entry # 29, Mitchell Point. From Hood River the total drivetime (there and back) is 15 minutes. It takes roughly 25 minutes to hike up, 20 minutes back down, and I figured 30 minutes of sightseeing at the top. 15+ 25+ 20+ 30= 90 minutes...wah-lah. From Portland the total drive is 110 minutes plus the 75 minutes for hiking 'n' hanging = 3 hour timeguess. Now take pi and multiply it by the radius squared... you get, ahh, yes Grasshoppah...the area of the circle. SEE, all this Gorge math is really easy if you're just willing to TRY!

DRIVING DIRECTIONS:

From Portland: since Portland traffic can now be an agonizing clusterfuck when you're trying to get out of the city to go play, the drivetime guess begins at the intersection of Hwys 205 and 84. You city-folk will have to bear the burden of figuring out how much time it will take you to get to this point, and add that to Curious George's drivetime guess. No monkeying around!

From Hood River: the directions assume that you are somewhere on Oak street, probably relaxed from all the small-town charm, elated at all the unbelievable shopping opportunities, amped-up from a Dog River Coffee expresso, and psyched to go play! Please use the Hood River map at the back of this guide to help steer you to your next adventure.

THE NW FOREST PASS:

This pass is required for parking at a bunch of trailheads throughout the Gorge. It isn't required to hike the actual trail, so if you park further away and walk in, you don't need to buy a pass. Enforcement is sometimes lax on weekdays, but at busy trailheads on weekends you can expect to be fined $50 if you don't have a pass. A day pass costs $5 and is available at most trailheads (if not, then I've tried to tell you where to get one). An annual pass is $30, which you can buy online at **naturenw.org** or at some Gorge retailers such as **Charburger** (in Cascade Locks) or **Second Wind** (in downtown Hood River). Call the Scenic Area office at 541-308-2750 for info or vendors.

Poison Oak Warning and Advice:

It's everywhere in the Gorge where there's lots of sun. It has 3-leaf clusters, little white berries under the leaves, and is shiny and reddish when it's most potent (late spring and summer). In Washington it's abundant because of the sun exposure. In Oregon it loves the clear-cuts under powerlines and sunny viewpoints.

Poison oak is worrisome, but with preparation you don't need to fear. Either wear long pants in the spring (when it's most active) or bring a kit in your car to clean up with. All you need is TECNU (available at Safeway, etc), some paper towels or sponge, and water. Keep it all in a big zip-lock bag. After a hike, when you're packing up the car, just wipe your exposed arms, legs, and hands with TECNU. Wait a minute then rinse and wipe it off. (If your girlfriend is with you, make sure you help her with all the wiping. Who knows where she may have gotten some Oak. It might be best to remove all her clothes so that you can Really Help Her!) Do it again if you're super-sensitive or paranoid. It works and it only takes 3 to 5 minutes. Don't wait until you get home where you keep a bottle in the shower. Inevitably you forget because you run into friends or get a burrito or something—then Whammo, 3 weeks of itch. **Do it at your car!!**

Also, be careful if you bring a dog. Dogs get covered with it then spread it to your car seats, your couch at home, and everyone who pets them.

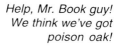

Help, Mr. Book guy! We think we've got poison oak!

The Hood River Time MATRIX

The author created The Matrix because it is what he wishes were contained in all the guidebooks he has read. When you are new to a town chances are that you don't have any idea how long it takes to get to all the places that you've heard about. Lost Lake looks closer the The Dalles, but how can you know that the road to the lake is super-curvy? How many times have you embarked on a slow dirt road and wished you actually knew how much time the drive takes rather than just how many miles? SO, here's this author's effort to help you...hope that it works!

The Matrix indexes both the time that an excursion takes to complete, round-trip from Hood River, and the features of the excursion. The time estimates range from a half-hour down to six hours. Built into these time estimates are some leisure time—the estimates **are not** the bare minimum required.

But here are a couple of generalizations; 1) The top third of the matrix is skewed towards a hurried-up, time constrained visit. This means that if you've got a tight schedule, then you're probably not out to mosey, photo, and snack. Thus, the time guess for #43, Catherine Creek is only one hour...hardly time to dawdle, but time enough to see the whole place and get back if you have another obligation. Or, take #19, Dog Creek Falls... the time guess is about 1.5 hours—that's enough for a drive and a look-see, but definitely not enough for a good exploration. Thus, the top third of the entries don't have much leisure time built in—they are meant to get you to see as much as you can on limited time!

On the other hand, the bottom third of the entries are skewed the opposite way. They build in more leisure time because if you've gone on an all-day hike or a long outing, then surely you're not in a big hurry. For example, #49 White River Falls... you could drive there, look, and return in 2.5 hours, but the time guess is about 4.5 hours because most folks go to swim and sunbathe and explore. At #36 Lost Lake, the guess is 4 hours—that's 2.5 hours actually at the lake.

The matrix is also a quick reference for a specific type of feature. You can scan down a column to find a hike with mountain views or maybe you want to see which excursions feature some exploration. Or maybe you just want to know which places are the quickest drive or which places don't have fees—quickquick, just scan a column!

Hail the Matrix!!

Roundtrip Time Estimate from Hood River (includes drive)

Hood River's Time Estimate MATRIX

Roundtrip Time	Destination	Scenic Hike	Waterfall	Columbia Views	Mtn Views	Exploration	Attraction	Drive Time (one-way)	Fee
.5 hr	Panorama Point Vwpt (34)				●		●	5	
	Cook-UnderW Rd Vwpt (23)			●	●		●	9	
	Mosier Creek Falls (38)	●	●				●	9	
	Northwestern Lake (21)						●	15	
	Starvation Creek Falls (27)		●			●		17	
	Condit Dam (22)	●				●	●	13	
	Hood River Museum (31)						●	1	
	Catherine Crk Falls Stroll (43)	●	●	●				15	
1 hr	Hist Col R. Hwy (33)	●		●				4	●
	Rainbow Garden (32)	●				●		2	
	Shellrock Mt Wagon Rd (26)			●		●		14	
	Punchbowl Falls (35)		●				●	17	
	Rowena Plateau Trail (39)	●		●				18	
	Courtney Road Viewpoint (41)			●	●		●	25	
	Gorton Creek Falls (25)		●			●		15	●
	Dog Creek Falls (19)		●			●		13	
	Mitchell Point Trail (29)	●		●				9	
	Wygant Trail (30)	●		●				9	
1.5 hrs	Catherine Crk Arch Trail (44)	●		●				15	
	Klickitat Gorge Salmon (45)	●					●	17	
	Indian Vision Quest Trail (42)	●		●		●		14	
	Cherry Orchard Trail (46)	●		●				17	
	Wahclella Falls Trail (7)	●	●					23	
	Panther Creek Falls (16)		●			●		40	
	Starvation Ridge Falls Trail (28)	●	●	●				17	
2 hrs	Oneonta Gorge (3)		●			●		30	
	Beacon Rock Trail (11)	●		●				30	●
	Bonneville Dam (6)						●	24	
	Ice Cave (20)					●		40	
	McCall Point Trail (40)	●		●	●			18	
	Elowah Falls Trail (5)	●	●	●				28	
	Hamilton Mountain Trail–Short (12)	●	●					30	●
	Horsethief Butte (47)	●		●		●	●	28	
	Tamanawas Falls Trail (37)	●	●					25	●
	Trapper Crk Trail- Loop (14)	●						40	●
	Wind Mountain Trail (17)	●		●	●			20	
3 hrs	Columbia Gorge Interp Ctr (13)						●	25	
	Columbia Gorge Disc Ctr (48)						●	20	
	Dry Creek Falls Trail (9)	●	●					22	●
	Wygant/Chetwoot Trail–Loop (30)	●		●				9	
	Eagle Creek Trail (8)	●	●					25	●
	Latourell Falls Trail (1)	●	●	●				55	
	Falls Creek Falls Trail–Short (15)	●	●					43	●
	Multnomah/Wahkeena Trail (2)	●	●	●				32	
	Cape Horn Trail (10)	●	●	●				45	
4 hrs	Five Falls Loop Trail (4)	●	●	●				30	
	Lost Lake (36)	●					●	45	●
	White River Falls (49)		●			●		60	
	Dog Mountain Trail (18)	●		●	●			15	●
	Hamilton Mt. Trail–Summit (12)	●	●	●	●			30	●
	Indian Point Trail (24)	●		●				18	●
5 hrs	Falls Creek Falls Trail–Loop (15)	●	●			●		43	●
	Trapper Crk Tr-Soda Peaks L (14)	●						40	●
	Eagle Creek–Tunnel Falls (8)	●	●					25	●

Hiking Difficulty Scale

This scale lists every hike in the guide from easiest to most difficult. The purpose is to help you understand how your personal fitness and hiking ability relates to the Curious Gorge rating.

For example: Hike Tamanawas Falls. It's rated as moderate. You might think that it was super-easy or you might think, wow, that was tough. If you thought the hike was easy, then you now know that a Curious Gorge 'moderate' is easy for you. On the other hand, if you think the hike was very hard, now you know to expect more difficulty on any hike further down the scale. **Also,** you can use this scale if you have a visitor with hiking issues and you just want a quick run-down of the easiest hikes in the guide (or the toughest)—without having to leaf through the pages or scan the Matrix.

Easiest	Historic Columbia River Hwy Trail (33)
	Klickitat River Gorge Salmon Spawning (45)
	Catherine Creek Falls Stroll (43)
	Rowena Plateau Trail (39)
	Condit Dam (22)
	Rainbow Garden (32)
	Mosier Creek Falls/Pioneer Cemetery (38)
	Horsethief Butte (47)
	Wahclella Falls Trail (7)
	Lost Lake Loop (36)
	Beacon Rock Trail (11)
	Hamilton Mountain- Easy (12)
	Indian Vision Quest Pits Trail (42)
	Latourell Falls Trail (1)
	Elowah Falls Trail (5)
	Wygant Trail (short) (30)
Moderate	Catherine Creek Arch Trail (44)
	Dry Creek Falls Trail (9)
	Eagle Creek Trail (8)
	Trapper Creek Old Growth Loop (14)
	Falls Creek Falls- Short (15)
	Tamanawas Falls Trail (37)
	Wygant/ Chetwoot Loop (30)
	Multnomah/ Wahkeena Loop (2)
	Five Falls Loop Trail (4)
	McCall Point Trail (40)
	Starvation Ridge Waterfalls Trail (28)
	Mitchell Point Trail (29)
	Cape Horn Trail (10)
	Cherry Orchard Trail (46)
	Wind Mountain Trail (17)
Hardest	Falls Creek Falls- Loop (15)
	Hamilton Mountain- Summit (12)
	Indian Point Trail (24)
	Trapper Creek- Soda Peaks Lake (14)
	Dog Mountain Trail (18)

10 COOL PLACES ON HOT DAYS

White River Falls (49)
Punchbowl Falls (35)
Oneonta Gorge (3)
Dog Creek Falls (19)
Hamilton Mtn Trail–Short (12)
Starvation Creek Falls (27)
Panther Creek Falls (16)
Mosier Creek Falls (38)
Ice Cave (20)
Gorton Creek Falls (25)

KIDS LOVE...

Mosier Creek Falls (38)
Lost Lake (36)
Ice Cave (20)
Northwestern Lake (21)
White River Falls (49)
Horsethief Butte (47)
Beacon Rock Trail (11)
Bonneville Dam (6)
Dog Creek Falls (19)
Hamilton Mtn Trail- Short (12)
Rainbow Garden (32)

WILDFLOWER CHASING

April to mid-May:
Horsethief Butte (7)
Catherine Crk Falls Stroll (43)
Rowena Plateau Trail (39)
McCall Point Trail (40)
Cherry Orchard Trail (46)
Indian Vision Quest Trail (42)

mid-May thru June:
Dog Mountain Trail (18)
Wygant/ Chetwoot Trail (30)
Hist Col River Hwy (33)
Panorama Point (34)

July:
Hamilton Mt. Trail (4)
Cape Horn Trail (10)

SOME GREAT BOOKS ABOUT THE GORGE

Cataclysms on the Columbia, by Allen and Burns

Great story of Harlen Bretz and his battle to get his catacysmic "Missoula Flood" theories accepted as fact...as well as a geologic overview of how the floods shaped the Gorge.

Bridge of the Gods, Mountains of Fire, by Chuck Williams

History of the Columbia's Indians and their culture and how the coming of the white men has changed the Columbia in the last 220 years.

A River Lost, by Blaine Harden

An engaging and easy-to-read look at the modern Columbia River and the battles that wage over salmon/barging/recreation/Hanford/hydroelectric power/irrigation/cultures/environment. Brilliant!!!

Fire at Eden's Gate (Tom McCall and the Oregon Story), by Brent Walth

The story of Gov. Tom McCall. SO GOOD! Anyone who loves Oregon should read this book. This riveting biography recounts why Oregon rose to national prominence in the '70s do to McCall's maverick, innovative, and farsighted form of Governing. **Read this book!!**

100 Hikes in NW Oregon, by William Sullivan

Sullivan writes the best hiking books that Oregon has ever seen.

The Columbia: America's Great Highway, by Sam Lancaster

Astounding collection of Scenic Hwy photos—wow! (New $12.95 paperback)

The Magnificent Gateway, by John Eliot Allen

A geologic overview (in easy-to-understand language) of the Gorge from a pre-eminent Portland geologist.

Even though this guide is primarily for active hiking and exploring, there's also plenty included for folks not fit for much legging-it. Are your grandparents visiting? How about a brother or sister with their young kids? Maybe you just want to take it easy....

DRIVING TOUR of Historic Highway "waterfall alley"
(page 16 and entries 1-4) (don't miss Multnomah Falls Lodge and Crown Point Vista House).

VISIT:
Bonneville Dam (entry 6).
Columbia Gorge Interpretive Center (entry 13).
Hood River Museum (entry 31).
Columbia Gorge Discovery Center (entry 48).

STROLL:
Historic Hwy state trail (entry 33)
Catherine Creek's paved wildflower path (entry 43).
Rowena Plateau's wildflowers (entry 39).

DRIVE to these viewpoints:
Panorama Point (entry 34)
Cook-Underwood road (entry 23)
Courtney road (entry 41)
Cape Horn (entry 10)

PICNIC at:
Lost Lake (entry 36)
Northwestern Lake (entry 21)
Starvation Falls (entry 27)

VIEW:
Petroglyph display at Columbia Hills state park (entry 47)

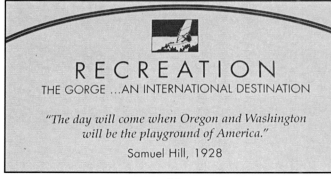

RECREATION
THE GORGE ...AN INTERNATIONAL DESTINATION

"The day will come when Oregon and Washington will be the playground of America."

Samuel Hill, 1928

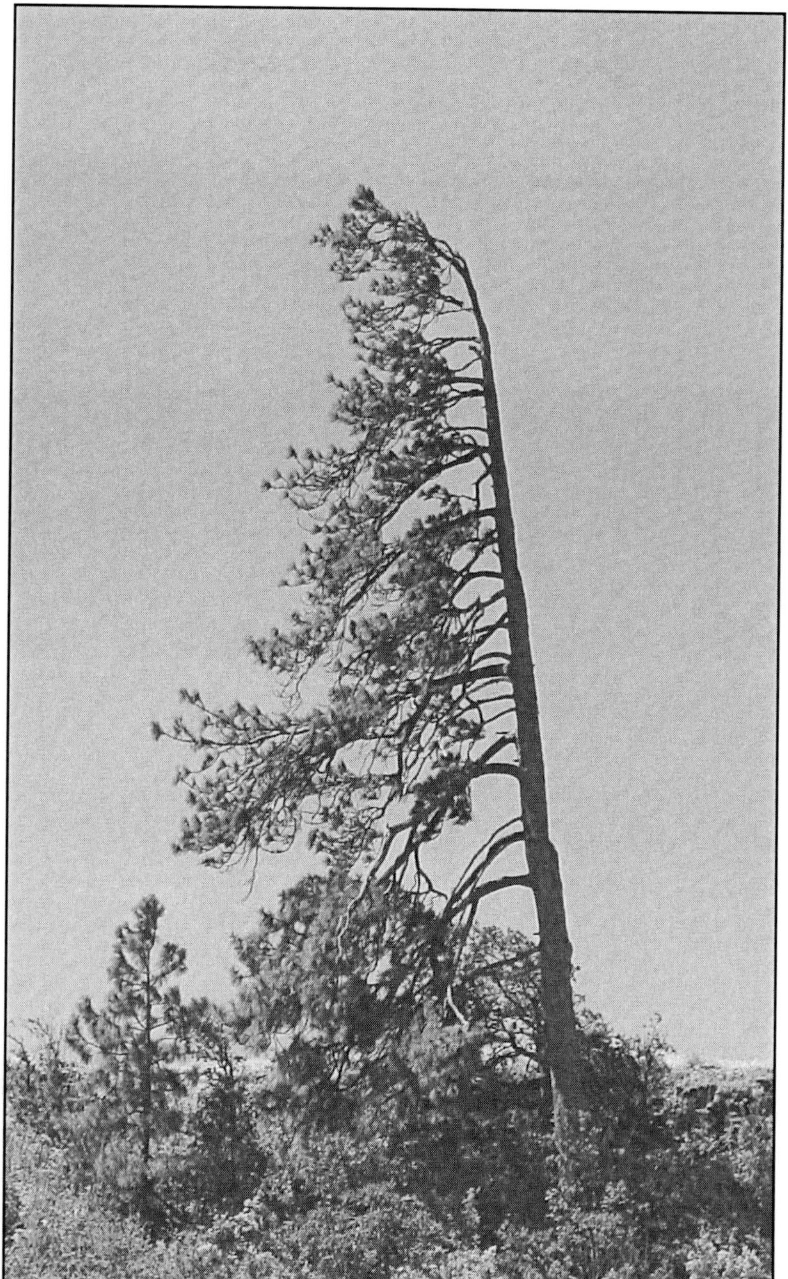

"Waterfall Alley" at a Glance: Oregon's most scenic 13 miles!

The Historic Columbia River Highway from Corbett to Dodson

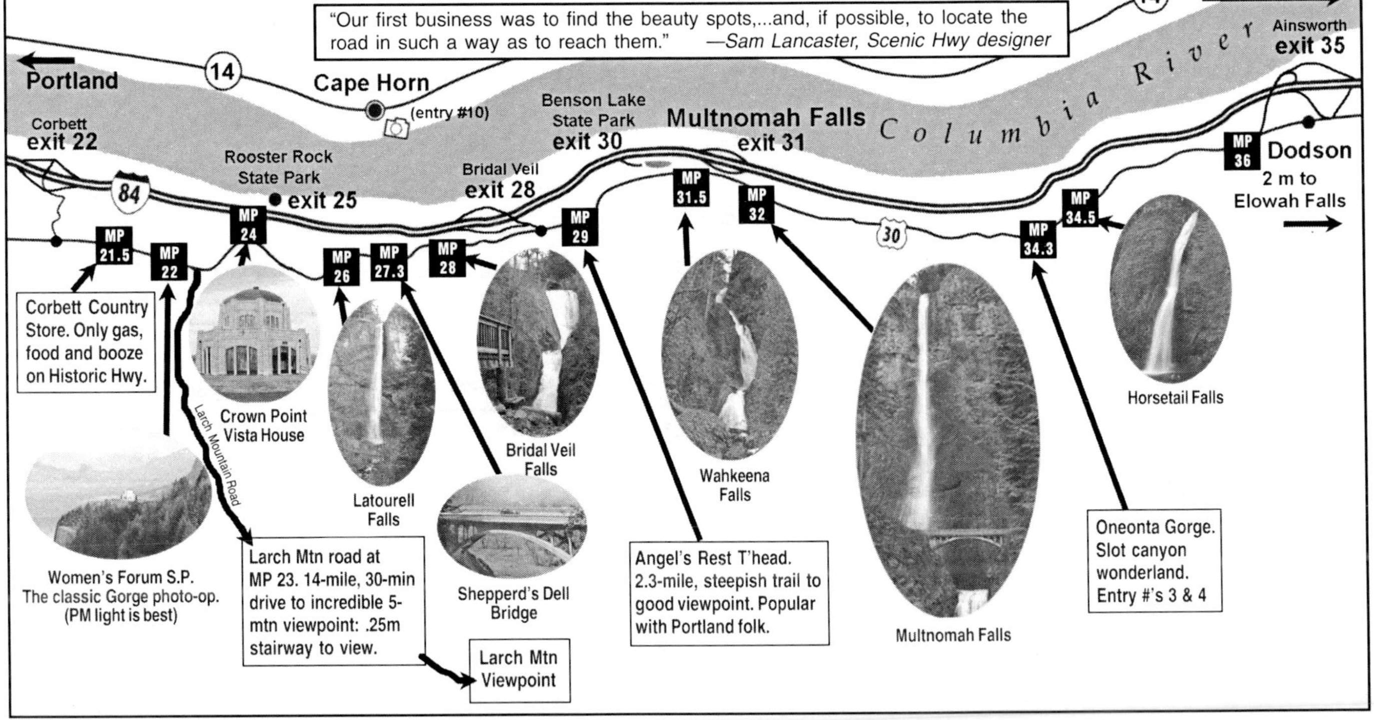

The Columbia River Highway, built by hand 1913-15, was the dream and accomplishment of Sam Hill and Sam Lancaster. It was heralded worldwide as one of the greatest engineering feats of the age. At the time of the highway's 1916 dedication (by Pres. Woodrow Wilson), international newspapers lauded the new highway as "The King of Roads" as well as "A Poem in Stone". The Scenic Highway shone as the nation's newest diamond!

The Historic Highway can be confusing these days (shine on, you crazy diamond)...**READ THIS:**

- The MP #s (in black above) are the Hist. Hwy mileage markers. Refer to entries 1-5 to hike and explore beyond the obvious sights.
- Multnomah Falls/ Lodge is the centerpiece. It has its own I-84 exit #31. This exit/parking has only foot-access to the Falls—you can't drive onto the Hist. Hwy from this exit.
- Corbett exit #22 is the **BEST way to access the Hist. Hwy coming from Portland.** It's a both-ways on/off exit, and it leads you quickly up to MP 22, just west of Crown Point.
- Bridal Veil exit #28 is a limited exit—only eastbound/off westbound/on. From Portland only take this exit to get to Multnomah fast.
- Ainsworth exit #35 is both ways on/off. Use this exit to start/end your tour.

Drivetime info: between I-84 exits #28 and #35 the Hist. Hwy. is relatively straight and fast. Between exits #22 and #28 the Hist. Hwy. is slow and curvy as it climbs 700 feet to Crown Point.

Larch Mtn road, at MP 22, leads 14 miles to an exquisite viewpoint, but it's a 30-min drive one-way, and at least 1.5 hours roundtrip to enjoy the view. Get snacks at Corbett store before you go!

Hey, read this! The author worked hard to squeeze all these adjectives into one sentence.

So, here's Oregon's Garden of Eden: unforgettable natural beauty—towering waterfalls, lush forest, cliff-edge views, sheer basalt canyons and ramparts—all highlighted by graceful bridges, intricate stonework, and inspired design. Rand McNally awards it one of the top 10 scenic roads in the country...ENJOY!!

Scenic Hike/Waterfalls

1

Roundtrip time-guess from Portland: 2 hours
from Hood River: 3 hours

Difficulty level: Easy photo-op or easy/mod 2 mile loop
Highlights: Gorgeous waterfall, secret trail

Latourell Falls Trail

Hey, want a tasty easy/mod 2m loop trail that features sumptuous views of sublimely beautiful Latourell Falls and its "secret" upstream sister? Well, don't look for signs at the waterfall's trailhead…'cuz there aren't any. Curious, but true…as of 4/06.

Latourell Falls is the Gorge's first major waterfall for those coming from Portland. Everybody stops there after seeing Crown Point. But, at the parking area there is no mention of either a loop trail or an upper falls, so only savvy guidebook owners would know that the trail makes a really great scenic loop. Most folks simply walk down the path to see "big" Latourell then turn back to continue their HCRH sightseeing cruise… bahhh, poor sheep. A trip upstream tours some big old-growth, the two-tiered upper falls, a Columbia viewpoint, and ends by leading under the highway bridge to the sweet creek side photo-op of big Latourell. Hooo… pretty big bang for your 2-mile bucks.

No B&W photo can do justice to Latourell's charm. The hyper-yellow lichen and columnar basalt dazzle!

DRIVING: **From Hood River:** Take I-84 west. Since Bridal Veil is an eastbound-only exit, you must continue to Corbett exit 22. At exit go left and up the hill for 1.5 miles to the Hist Hwy. Go left onto Hist Hwy and follow it 4 miles (passing Women's Forum and Crown Point) to Latourell parking (MP 26).

- Drivetime from Portland: 25 min
- from Hood River: 55 min
- Fee: free
- Restroom: yes

From Portland: Take I-84 east to Bridal Veil exit 28. Turn right onto the Hist. Hwy and follow it back west for 2 miles (passing Bridal Veil and Shepperd's Dell) to Latourell's large parking lot.

HIKE: The best views come from doing the loop clockwise. Head up the steep paved path, pass the viewpoint and continue up to the top of the falls. From here the trail heads upstream for .5m, crosses a bridge at the upper falls, then comes back on the other side for .5m. Take the righthand fork to a nice viewpoint (a rocky scramble lets you peer over the falls and across the Columbia to the Cape Horn cliffs (entry 10)). Continue down another .5m, cross the highway, descend some stairs, then turn right onto the paved path that soon crosses under the bridge to the Falls' base and then back up to parking.

Everyone can visit the lower creek

NOTE: A less-venturesome and all-paved .5m loop is also possible. Head down to the Falls, keep going under bridge then turn left at the picnicground. Climb steeply up to the highway and turn left to cross bridge back to parking.

Sam and Daphne, visiting from Tennessee, stop for a smooch at the upper falls

Scenic Hike/Waterfalls/Columbia Views

2

Roundtrip time-guess from Portland: 3 hours
from Hood River: 3 hours

Difficulty level: moderate 5-mile loop
Highlights: Oregon's signature waterfall

Multnomah/Wahkeena Falls Trail

The catch-22 of Multnomah's beauty

AHH, Multnomah Falls… the Gorge's signature icon. 620 feet of WOW visited annually by an estimated 2.5 million people. Expect a crowd and you'll still love a visit. Expect wilderness and you'll probably freak-out at the summertime crowd of overweight expresso drinkin', hot-dog munchin', ice-cream lickin' masses that lounge around at the waterfall's concession area.

But wait, what can a solitude-loving guidebook author enjoy amidst Multnomah's throngs? Well, probably **one of the Gorge's most beautiful loop hikes!** Yup, a 5-mile route heads up to Multnomah's top then cuts west over to the top of Wahkeena creek. You then descend this gorgeous creek back to the highway and then cruise a half-mile back to Multnomah. This hike is fantastic—two superlative creeks plus many other waterfalls and surprises in one neat package! The crowds that swarm to the top of Multnomah mostly all turn back as you continue up above the falls. The upper creek trail feels magical as it passes two 50-foot falls. Then, crossing to Wahkeena, you can take a 100-step detour to see Wahkeena's surprising trailside spring—whoa, the creek emerges full-blown from the hillside… Neat! The cruise down Wahkeena creek is charming—it's a super-steep moss-a-rama. You get to skip in front of Fairy Falls, navigate down the well-switchbacked trail to the Wahkeena Bridge photo-op, then end up back on the Hist. Hwy.

Upper Multnomah Creek

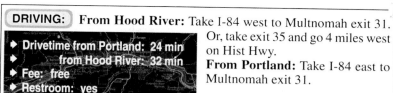

DRIVING: **From Hood River:** Take I-84 west to Multnomah exit 31. Or, take exit 35 and go 4 miles west on Hist Hwy.
From Portland: Take I-84 east to Multnomah exit 31.

- Drivetime from Portland: 24 min
- from Hood River: 32 min
- Fee: free
- Restroom: yes

NOTE: For first-time visitors...the steep, paved one-mile trail to Multnomah's top is super-crowded with smokers, strollers, and cell-phone chatters. The view platform at the top really isn't too scenic, except of the parking lot. A better nearby short hike would be up to Ponytail Falls (entry 4).

HIKE: You could do this hike up Wahkeena first, but it is better to hike this loop up Multnomah first—better to start with a crowd than end with one.

The secrets of Mult. Creek

Head up Mult. .2m to bridge then a steep .7m more to the top. After viewpoint head upstream .75m more and then turn right onto Wahkeena trail #420. In about .7m more you'll come to a 3-way junction. Both forks direct 1.9m down to Hwy, but go left because it's better (100 yards down this trail stop and listen for the curious gurgling spring which sounds the origin of Fairy Falls' stream—you'll pass the stream and see the falls on the way down). In .3m arrive at Angel's Rest junction. Before descending, go left for 100 steps to see Wahkeena's spring. Head back and down Wahkeena for 1.6m to Hwy and pick up trail # 424 that heads .5m back to Multnomah.

Fairy Falls

Wahkeena Falls

Exploration/Waterfall

3

Roundtrip time-guess from Portland: 2 hours
from Hood River: 2 hours

Difficulty level: Mod/diff .3 miles one-way
Highlights: Creekbed scramble thru slot canyon

Oneonta Gorge

Grab your galoshes cuz yer gonna get wet! Oneonta Gorge is a gasp-inspiring marvel—it's a narrow slot canyon carved between towering 200-foot walls. 'Tis a true botanical Wonderland... emerald green mosses...colorful lichen...plants and flowers found nowhere else in the world. And the final exclamation point of this fun-to-explore chasm is the view around the last bend—the magnificent 60-foot Oneonta Falls. Truly one of the most unique areas in all the Columbia River Gorge, and probably America. How many other basalt slot canyons with hidden waterfalls exist?? Gotta love the Gorge!

DRIVING:

- Drivetime from Portland: 30 min
- from Hood River: 30 min
- Fee: free
- Restroom: no

From Hood River: Take I-84 west to Ainsworth exit 35. Go straight onto the Hist Hwy. Drive 2 miles west, passing Horsetail Falls, and pull off at either side of the Oneonta Creek bridge.
From Portland: Take I-84 east to exit 35. Follow above directions.

Oneonta Falls

EXPLORE: From the parking area start on the left side of the creek. There is no real trail in the 0.3 mile long canyon. The trail is the Oneonta Creek itself. To reach the falls you must first scramble over a couple of huge log jams and then splash and wade your way upstream through the pebbled creekbed. **Good footwear or water sandals are a must, as are shorts or a swimsuit…you will get wet!** It's possible to hike almost to the waterfall with only wet feet, but the falls are hidden around a bend just past a 40-foot section of thigh-deep water. Definitely get to the falls—they're worth the wetness!

Scenic Hike/Waterfalls/Columbia Views

4

Roundtrip time-guess from Portland: 4 hours
from Hood River: 4 hours

Difficulty level: Mod. 2.7-mile loop with 2-mile extension
Highlights: Waterfalls, canyons, and viewpoints

Five Waterfalls Loop Trail

This nice 2.7 mile loop (with a 2-mile side-trip) features 5 different waterfalls, cliff-edge viewpoints, and a wet exploration of the surreal Oneonta Gorge. The visual pleasures on this trail make it one of the best hikes in the whole Gorge! The hiking is easy on this wide and well-groomed trail. Unique highlights include a walk behind Ponytail Falls, a rare view of bald eagle habitat, and a peek from above into Oneonta Gorge. Also, a 1.0 mile side-trail option goes to 120-foot Triple Falls then descends back to the highway to complete the 4.7 mile loop. Back at the highway you'll now splash up Oneonta Creek to see the magnificent slot canyon and final waterfall!

The trail cuts behind Ponytail Falls

DRIVING: **From Hood River:** Take I-84 west to Ainsworth exit 35. Go straight onto the Hist Hwy. Drive 2 miles west, passing Horsetail Falls, and pull off at either side of the Oneonta Creek bridge.

From Portland: Take I-84 east to exit 35. Follow above directions.

- **Drivetime from Portland: 30 min**
- **from Hood River: 30 min**
- **Fee: free**
- **Restroom: no**

HIKE: (There's a map at Horsetail showing the route) From Oneonta, walk east on the Historic Hwy 0.3 miles to Horsetail Falls. Begin the trail on the left side of the falls. Climb to Ponytail Falls, staying right at the trail junction. Walk behind Ponytail and continue to the viewpoint area where short spur trails lead to unguarded perches. Now continue towards Oneonta Creek. This is the bald eagle habitat—look out across the canyon and you may see a treetop nest or possibly the eagles themselves! Descend a bit to a view into Oneonta Gorge and then down to the bridge next to the third waterfall, Upper Oneonta Falls. After the bridge switchback up to another trail junction. *This is the side-trip option:Go left here on trail 424 for 1.0 miles to see Triple Falls (the trail continues all the way to Larch Mountain, but Triple Falls is your destination for this hike).* From Triple, retrace your steps, pass the junction, and stay on Trail 424 to the hwy. A trail spurs off to the right and rejoins in a few hundred yards—if you want another Columbia view. At the hwy go right, back to your car. Change clothes and scramble into Oneonta Gorge to see the fifth falls—the hidden Oneonta Falls (see previous entry). Rejoice! If you forgot your cooler, the Multnomah Lodge, 2 miles west, serves beer and wine.

Triple Falls

Scenic Hike/Waterfalls/Columbia Views

5

Roundtrip time-guess from Portland: 2.5 hours
from Hood River: 2.5 hours

Difficulty level: easy/mod .75-mile to falls, 1 mile to top, 3.5 miles for both

Highlights: Little-known major waterfall

Elowah Falls Trail

Elowah may be the most overlooked major waterfall in the whole Gorge. This gem gracefully leaps from a notch in the cliff and falls for an impressive 290 feet...often for your eyes only. Whereas Multnomah Falls may have 6,000 - 10,000 visitors on a summer day, Elowah may only see 10 - 20 people on the same day. The main reason is that the parking lot/ trailhead is weirdly hard to find—it's not on the Historic Hwy waterfall circuit, but it is just a few miles east of Horsetail Falls. Hmmm...you've just got to beat off the main path a bit! No crowds, all the better.

Elowah Falls, the Gorge's most overlooked

Twin Falls

A well-made trail leads .75m to the base of the waterfall—careful, your jaw may drop in witness of Elowah's majesty. The cascade drops into the very center of a huge basalt amphitheater! Explore the misty pool or chase a rainbow across the creek bridge to the boulders.

Before you descend to the falls' base though, take the "Upper McCord Falls" spur trail that leads about a mile up to the top of Elowah and then deadends at Upper McCord's twin falls. This trail is sweet… as you near the top the trail is carved into the wall and protected by guardrails. Revel in Gorge views, including Beacon Rock, while seeing Elowah pour into its basin below you. **The best way to love Elowah is to visit the top first (full of energy and anticipation), then descend to the base for snacks and frolicking.**

DRIVING: **From Hood River:** Take I-84 west to Warrendale exit 37. Take exit and go .3 miles then left under the Hwy, then left again. Go .3 miles back east and pull into the Yeon trailhead before re-entering Hwy.

From Portland: Take I-84 east to Ainsworth exit 35. At stop go left, then immediately right onto Frontage road and follow it 2 miles to Yeon parking.

HIKE: Stay left at the immediate Nesmith junction. In less than a half mile you'll come to the Upper McCord junction—either head up or continue on to the base. The trail continues past Elowah, but there's not much to see for a long way. Turn back at falls.

Pam gazes from the upper McCord trail's viewpoints

Gorge Attraction

6

Roundtrip time-guess from Portland: 3 hours
from Hood River: 2.5 hours

Difficulty level: easy
Highlights: Visitor center, fish viewing windows, sturgeon ponds

Bonneville Dam

The first dam on the Columbia, finished in 1938, is a fun and informative place– part museum, part hydroelectric engine, and part aquarium. The Bonneville Visitor Center, Lock, and Hatchery lend excellent perspective to the complexity of our mighty Columbia River. As Woody Guthrie sings over the speaker system, "Roll on Columbia, your power is turning our darkness to dawn…".

At the **Visitor Center** view a collection of historical photos and videos of both the pre-dam and post-dam eras. Interesting displays about the numerous dams along the Columbia help to show their role in our modern times. Head downstairs to see the super-popular fish ladder viewing windows. Watch salmon and steelhead by the hundreds race by on their journey upriver. Education panels detail the life cycle of the salmon and the conservation efforts being made to increase their numbers.

At the **Locks**, if you're lucky, you can witness the passage of a barge either up or down the river—quite impressive! *Note: the locks have been closed to visitation since 9/11/01—security issues.*

No stop is complete without checking out the **Hatchery**. This hatchery has rearing ponds full of fingerling smolts, but it also has a sort of outdoor aquarium where you can feed sturgeon and steelhead in their ponds. A machine dispenses fish food for 25¢— kids love it! Best by far is 'Herman' the legendary monster sturgeon. His pond, at the east end of the grounds, has a huge underwater viewing window. It's a hoot to see first-time visitors gape in awe as he makes an appearance—he's quite the ham.

Herman's Aquarium

DRIVING:

- Drivetime from Portland: 33 min
- from Hood River: 24 min
- Open year-round 9-5pm
- Fee: free
- Restroom: yes

From Hood River: Take I-84 west to Bonneville exit 40. Turn right towards the dam. The hatchery is the left fork and the visitor center is straight past the guard booth.

From Portland: Take I-84 east to Bonneville exit 40.

The roar and mist of the dam spillways

Scenic Hike/Waterfall

7

Roundtrip time-guess from Portland: 2 hours
from Hood River: 1.75 hours

Difficulty level: easyish 1-mile one-way
Highlights: Thundering chasm at end of short hike

Wahclella Falls Trail

A superb one-mile trail traipses into the very heart of the Gorge...at the same exit as the Bonneville Dam. Like those fruit bars concocted of the Hood River Valley's bounty, this hike is a true Gorge delight!

The easy-ish 1.0m trail follows Tanner Creek upstream and then ends at the base of thundering Wahclella Falls. This waterfall is one of the Gorge's most scenic and the trail is a delight also. You begin on the short gravel road up to the Bonneville hatchery's water intake dam, then quickly turn a corner to a surprise. ☺ Heading upstream, the gurgle of the creek accents towering canyon walls, lush mosses, and sporadic old-growth... mmmm mmm good!

Thunderous chasm

There's a little loop at the end of the trail—go right and down for the best ahhhs. As you cross the bridge notice all the boulders and jumbled rocks. The forest service reports that a landslide in 1973 brought all this rock down from the western walls. Notice how no big trees are growing yet on the landslide talus compared to the adjacent slopes. Now, continue on to the second bridge and Wahclella's grandeur!

This trail is a year-round joy, but it may be best in the fall when salmon choke the stream by the dam, the maple leaves have fallen revealing better views, and the seasonal waterfall above Wahclella's slot is beginning to charge.

DRIVING: **From Hood River:** Take I-84 west for 22 miles to Bonneville exit 40. At the bottom of the ramp go left then right at the "T" to the trailhead.

From Portland: Take I-84 east to Bonneville exit 40. Go right to trailhead.

- **Drivetime from Portland: 33 min**
- **from Hood River: 23 min**
- **Fee: NW Forest Pass @ T'head**
- **Restroom: yes**

The landslide area

HIKE: No directions needed. One mile to falls with short loop at end

NOTE: At the trailhead entrance you can head left up the road to the Tooth Rock trailhead. This is an easy one-mile paved section of the Historic Hwy that showcases some nice views as well as the Hwy viaduct and its photogenic curvy moss-covered stone guardrails.

Creekside serenity begins this hike

Scenic Hike/Waterfalls

8

Roundtrip time-guess from Portland: 3 to 5 hours
from Hood River: 3 to 5 hours

Difficulty level: easy/mod 1.5 to 6 miles one-way
Highlights: Classic Gorge canyon chock-full-o-falls

Eagle Creek Trail

The Eagle Creek trail is probably the Gorge's "classic" hike. If there is one trail in the Gorge with international credentials, this is it! Greg Plumb, author of the definitive "Waterfall Lovers Guide to the Northwest" calls this trail "his favorite single hike." In fact, it seems to be everyone's favorite, so beware daunting summertime crowds.

The reasons for Eagle Creek's fame are many. First, the canyon is a stunner—towering walls, towering old-growth, towering umph! Second, the plentiful waterfalls have international acclaim—Punchbowl has graced calenders and books the world over. And third, the trail itself is a marvel—'twas constructed around 1915, painstakingly hand-carved into the cliff walls in order to maintain a miraculously even grade as it winds upstream. Sweet!... no steep spots, no heavy breathing... great for the whole family... but dogs and children should be leashed because of the sheer drop-offs.

Idyllic Metlako Falls

DRIVING: **From Hood River:** Eagle Creek exit 41 is only accessible from I-84 eastbound. Take I-84 west to exit 40, get off and flip-flop back to eastbound exit 41.
From Portland: Take I-84 east to exit 41.

- **Drivetime from Portland: 34 min**
- **from Hood River: 25 min**
- **Fee: NW Forest Pass @ T'head**
- **Restroom: yes**

Punchbowl Falls (see page 4)

The entire trail is actually 14 miles to Wahtum Lake. You'll see plenty of backpackers heading to the upriver camp sites. Most day-hikers turn around much sooner. Probably 75% of summer hikers only go the first 1.5 miles to Punchbowl Falls to wade, swim, jump, photo, and picnic with all the like-minded folk. The next good turn-around point is High Bridge, at the 3-mile mark (just past pretty Loowit Falls). If you want to venture further than this, you should plan to go all the way to Tunnel Falls at the 6-mile mark. This 120-foot falls is so-named because the trail is carved through the basalt behind the falls—completely spectacular! And just steps beyond Tunnel Falls is another amazing cataract that has good creekside picnic spots just past it.

For Gorge locals, this canyon's beauty is best showcased fall through spring. No Crowds...maple leaves have fallen...diffused cloudy light...your eyes can really hone in on Eagle's secret nooks, mossy wonderlands, and hidden side-canyon waterfalls...so nice!

HIKE: No options or loops. Metlako Falls is at 1.0m, Punchbowl is at 1.5m, High Bridge at 3.0m, and Tunnel Falls at 6.0m.

HEY: Dave Grove, a Hood River kayaker, actually kayaked over 101-foot Metlako Falls on 5/9/04. Stop into the Kayak Shed in HR to see the impressive photo-poster!

The trail has scary drop-offs with helpful handrails

Scenic Hike/Waterfall

9

Roundtrip time-guess from Portland 3.5 hours
from Hood River: 2.75 hours

Difficulty level: easy/mod 2-mile one-way
Highlights: Pleasant hike to little-known falls

Dry Creek Falls Trail

An easy 2.0 mile section of the Pacific Crest Trail explores a lush forest on its way to the base of Dry Creek Falls. Even though you start at the obvious Bridge of the Gods trailhead, this trail is not very well known...mostly because there are no signs indicating the nice waterfall ahead. After five minutes of hiking the highway noise disappears, leaving only serenity as the trail contours along a canyon thick with ferns.

Pouring from a slot, Dry Creek Falls is a 70-foot horsetail cascade nestled between striking 200-foot high columnar basalt walls! At the base of the falls a lush fern oasis keeps you cool—making it a great venue to escape Gorge winds to a tranquil and isolated setting.

South entrance to Bridge of The Gods

DRIVING: **From Hood River:** Take I-84 west to Cascade Locks exit 44. Go straight 1.5 miles through town, and turn left at signs for the Bridge of the Gods. Turn right into the trailhead parking area just before the tollbooth.

- **Drivetime from Portland: 37 min**
- **from Hood River: 22 min**
- **Fee: NW Forest Pass (@ Charburger)**
- **Restroom: yes**

From Portland: Take I-84 east to Cascade Locks exit 44. At the end of the exit turn right towards the Bridge of the Gods then right again into the trailhead parking.

The inspiring solitude of Dry Creek Falls

HIKE: Start across the road from the restrooms at the signed trailhead—'Pacific Crest Trail/Gorge Trail 400'. The trail quickly goes beneath the highway. Stay right and go up the gravel road. In about 100 yards the trail branches both left and right off the road. Go left onto Pacific Crest Trail South into the forest. Soon you emerge under the powerlines. Go right and look for the trail as it resumes to the left off the dirt road. The next 1.5 miles are serene as you gradually climb to Dry Creek. Arriving at the creek there is a dirt road running alongside it and a bridge that goes over it. The bridge is the continuation of the Pacific Crest Trail on its way to Mexico, but for this hike go right, up the dirt road 0.25 miles to the waterfall. The dirt road does lead down into Cascade Locks, but it's convoluded—it's better to go back the way you came.

Scenic Hike/Columbia Views/Waterfall

10

Roundtrip time-guess from Portland: 3.5 hours
from Hood River: 3.5 hours

Difficulty level: mod/diff 1.75 miles one-way
Highlights: Unique cliff-edge views, secret waterfall

Cape Horn Trail

Explore this little-known rough trail as it descends from Hwy 14 down to some very unique cliff-edge viewpoints and then on to a sprinkly waterfall grotto.

Cape Horn's cliffs, rising dramatically out of the Columbia, have been a notable landmark on the river since Lewis and Clark times. C. E. Watkins, the Gorge's first photographer, beautifully captured these cliffs on his initial 1867 photo foray. River users pass close-by the cliffs daily, but most other folks only see them from I-84 in Oregon (just east of Rooster Rock). WA'ers know the Cape Horn viewpoint on Wash. Hwy 14.

Virtually nobody knows that there's a trail to explore these cliffs!! Some really dedicated "friends of the Gorge" have been working for years to construct and maintain a trail to help people visit this wonderful area...but, as yet, this is not an "officially" maintained forest service trail even though the land is public.

Highlights of this trail are a bunch of cliff-edge viewpoints, scads of early-summer wildflowers, and a shower-like waterfall. The viewpoints sport vistas up and down the Columbia

The Cape Horn cliffs seen from Oregon

DRIVING: **From Hood River:** Cross HR bridge and go left for 40 miles, or take I-84 to Cascade Locks, cross bridge and go left 16 miles. The Cape Horn viewpoint is at MP 25. The trail begins just .3 miles west of the viewpoint at a large left-side pulloff (just past the truck-tipping-over signs).

From Portland: Take I-205 towards Vancouver and then take Hwy 14 east for 20 miles. Climb grade to MP 24. Start down and .6 miles beyond MP 24, at a sharp right curve, you'll pull off into a large right-side pulloff. Trail starts near the east end. If you get to the viewpoint, you've gone too far.

- **Drivetime from Portland: 45 min**
- **from Hood River: 45 min**
- **Fee: free**
- **Restroom: no**

Waterfall Grotto

and one even features a trickling waterfall directly above the train tunnel—it makes a great sunny spot to contemplate the beauties of the Gorge while waiting to be surprised by a train emerging from the tunnel. And then, whoa, the finale of the trail is sweet! The little creek that you hear at the start of the hike now hurtles over the upper cliff into a basalt grotto. The sprinkling creek falls about twelve feet away from the wall into a rock-floored pool. Ooh-la-la…it's just the perfect place to strip off your sweaty clothes for a joyous sunny skinnydip shower! Flip-flops really help the tender-footed and noon-3pm sun is best.

NOTE: From the waterfall the trail continues .7m to a private road—there are no more views nor a good way to loop. The Friends of the Gorge are ever-diligently planning a future loop trail, but for now turn back and re-visit the beauty spots on the way back up.

HIKE: The trail begins at the east end of the pullout. Start down and at the 4-way intersection head straight to check out the first view. Turn back from this viewpoint and now head west as the trail descends for about a mile to the first lower cliff perch. Follow along the cliffs and then climb a bit until you find the waterfall. Return the way you came.

Sailboat heading upriver under viewpoint

Scenic Hike/Gorge Landmark/Columbia Views

11

Roundtrip time-guess from Portland: 2.5 hours
from Hood River: 2 hours

Difficulty level: easy 1.0-miles one-way
Highlights: Great views from gorge landmark

Beacon Rock Trail

Rising 848 feet above the Columbia River, Beacon Rock is the basalt core of an eroded volcano. Winding to the top of this famous Gorge landmark (look for it in photos of Crown Point) is an easy 1.0 mile trail laboriously hand-built around 1916 by the rock's owner, Henry Biddle. Interpretive signs in the parking area detail an interesting history. Lewis and Clark explored and named this landmark and it's said to be the second largest freestanding monolith in the world—next to the Rock of Gibraltar. The trail is an engineering curiosity—kids love it! Built by hand with pick axes and burros, it alternates between switchbacks hewn into the basalt and terraced rampways cemented to the Rock, whoa! This hike is a joy for the whole family—the view from the top…Stevenson to Portland…is a real crowd-pleaser.

Looking east to Bonneville Dam

DRIVING: **From Hood River:** Take I-84 west to Cascade Locks exit 44. Go 1.5 miles, through town and turn left at signs to cross The Bridge of the Gods. Turn left onto Hwy 14 and proceed west 6.5 miles to the clearly marked parking area near MP 35. (**Or,** cross the HR bridge and go left on Hwy 14 for 30.0 miles.) **From Portland:** Take I-84 east to Cascade Locks exit 44. Turn right at the end of the exit to cross bridge and follow above directions.

- **Drivetime from Portland: 47 min**
- **from Hood River: 30 min**
- **Fee: $5 WA State Park @ T'head**
- **Restroom: yes**

From the Beacon Rock moorage you can see the trail's ramps (and maybe a bikini!)

HIKE: The easy, but sustained, 1.0 mile climb starts in deep forest and ends at the summit's guard-railed viewpoint. The signed trailhead is about 50 yards west of the parking/restroom area. There are no side trails or other options.

Trail rampways

Scenic Hike/Waterfalls/Columbia and Mountain Views

12

Roundtrip time-guess from Portland: 3 or 5 hours
from Hood River: 2.5 or 4.5 hours

Difficulty level: easy 1.25-mile one-way or diff 7.5-mile loop
Highlights: Unique waterfall picnic area, epic viewpoints

Hamilton Mountain Trails

Hamilton Mountain is the jutting ridge looming 2,400 feet over Beacon Rock and the Bonneville Dam. The trail options range in difficulty from an easy 2.5 mile out and back (suitable for children) to a challenging 7.5 mile loop for the more hardy. These hikes are distinctive because of an unusual waterfall, breathtaking cliffs, a 360° view at the summit, and a summer wildflower bonanza…in other words, Gorge nectar!

The hike begins as an easy/ moderate 1.25 mile graded trail to the 'Pool of Winds' waterfall area. This creekside area, nestled between the Rodney and Hardy waterfalls, is a popular place to picnic and sun yourself. The smooth rocks and gurgling serenade entice!

Option 2, continues past the waterfall another mile. It climbs a continuous set of switchbacks and a steep spur trail to a wildflowered cliff area. From these precipitous basalt cliffs you get a great view of the Bonneville Dam, Beacon Rock, the tip of Mt. Hood, and a long stretch of the Columbia. You'll want to turn around here if your time, energy or daylight is short.

Option 3, is the difficult loop. It's 1.0 more miles of steeps up to the arresting view at the summit of Hamilton Mtn. The Columbia stretches from Wind Mtn to Crown Point! Mt. Adams looms large and Mt. Hood shows its snowy peak. *(Notice the sheer Table Mtn to the east. Less than a 1,000 years ago a landslide from this mountain blocked and dammed the Columbia and gave rise to the legend of a land bridge, 'The Bridge of the Gods'.)* From the summit you'll return on the 3.5 mile 'backside trail' that rejoins the main trail near the waterfall.

Rodney Falls and 'Pool of Winds'

DRIVING: **From Hood River:** Take I-84 west to Cascade Locks exit 44. Go 1.5 miles, through town and turn left at signs to cross The Bridge of the Gods. Turn left onto Hwy 14 and proceed west 6.5 miles. At Beacon Rock turn right onto the State Park and Campground road and go up the road .3 miles and turn right into the first parking area. (**Or,** cross the HR bridge and go left on Hwy 14 for 30.0 miles.)

- Drivetime from Portland: 47 min
- from Hood River: 30 min
- Fee: $5 WA State Park @ T'head
- Restroom: yes

From Portland: Take I-84 east to Cascade Locks exit 44. Turn right at the end of the exit to cross bridge and follow above directions.

HIKE: The trailhead is behind the parking lot restrooms. Hike 1.25 miles to the waterfalls. Check out Hardy Falls then continue to the 'Pool of the Winds' area.

Turn back, or continue on **Option 2** by crossing the bridge and switchbacking to the Hardy/ Hamilton Mtn trail junction. Go right…over the next 0.75 miles there are some faint spurs, then a real definite spur trail that leads 100 feet out to a spectacular promontory. Just past this rocky perch is the unsigned ridge spur trail that rises steeply off the main trail. **Pay attention here, this spur trail is easy to miss.** It's initially steep, loose and rocky before it becomes a more defined trail to the cliffs. From the cliffs either turn back or continue along the ridge spur for **Option 3.** This overgrown path winds up and down on its way back to the main trail. Now go right for a final lungbusting 1.0 mile climb to the summit.

To finish the loop go north on the trail. Follow it down 1.0 miles to a wide viewpoint plateau. At the far end of the plateau head left down the gravel road 1.0 miles, following signs towards the campground and Hardy Creek Trail. Before crossing the creek go left onto the signed trail. In another 1.0 miles you'll reach the junction with the main trail. Go right and retrace your steps back to the parking area.

Looking down over Beacon Rock from the cliffs

Columbia Gorge Interpretive Center

Museum

13

Roundtrip time-guess from Portland: 3 hours
from Hood River: 2.5 hours

Difficulty level: easy
Highlights: Visual historic museum

This marvelous museum-like historic center overlooks the Gorge just west of Stevenson. It's a visual showcase of the Columbia River Gorge's amazing ancient and modern history. One automated slideshow depicts the cataclysmic geology of the area, while another slideshow focuses on the Gorge's future. Brilliant enlarged photographs relate 10,000 years of human history. Filling the main room are: a fishwheel replica, a restored logging truck, a basalt waterfall, and much more. A fantastic place to spend a couple of hours getting a feel for the dynamic past and present of the Gorge!

Museum entrance

DRIVING: **From Hood River:** Take I-84 west to Cascade Locks exit 44. Go 1.5 miles, through town and turn left at signs to cross The Bridge of the Gods. Turn right onto Hwy 14 and proceed east 1.5 miles. Turn left onto Rock Creek drive, pass Skamania Lodge entrance, and follow signs for the Interpretive Center. Once in the driveway, turn immediately right to the Center. (**Or,** cross the HR bridge and go left on Hwy 14 for 22.0 miles to Rock Creek drive at MP 43.)

From Portland: Take I-84 east to Cascade Locks exit 44. Turn right at the end of the exit to cross bridge and follow above directions.

- **Drivetime from Portland: 42 min**
- **from Hood River: 25 min**
- **Fee: adults $6**
- **Open year-round 10-5pm**
- **Restroom: yes**

Displays inside the main room

Scenic Hike/Old-Growth

14

Roundtrip time-guess from Portland: 4 hours or 5.5 hours
from Hood River: 2.5 hours or 5 hours

Difficulty level: easy 3.5-mile loop or diff 4.75-mile one-way
Highlights: Largest old-growth near Gorge

The largest forest of mature old-growth trees near the Gorge is at Trapper Creek Wilderness area. Old-growth in the Gorge is rare– not solely because of logging but also because of fire. Early in the 1900's fires such as the Yacolt Burn raged through the Gorge and old photos show hillsides of burned snags along the Columbia. Fortunately Mother Nature spared a few choice areas. The trees in Trapper Creek Wilderness are majestic! 300 to 500-year-old Douglas fir, western red cedar, and hemlock reach more than 300-feet tall. Wrapping your arms around an 8 to 10-foot trunk is awe-inspiring.

Gov't Mineral Springs Campground, located at the entrance to the wilderness area, was previously the site of a turn-of-the-century resort. The mineral spring that spawned the resort is still there—it's called "Iron Mike" and there is a hand pump that pumps the water into a drinking fountain…try it and see if it cures your ills, or causes you ill! From this free campground there are two trail options. Either a difficult 4.75 mile trek that relentlessly climbs 2,700 feet through old-growth up to Soda Peaks Lake, or an easy 3.5 mile loop hike featuring huge old-growth as well as a few creek crossings.

Creek-hopping in the old-growth jungle

DRIVING: **Drive from Hood River:** Cross the HR bridge and go left on Hwy 14 for 15.5 miles. Just past the Wind River bridge (near MP 50) turn right onto Hot Springs Ave. Go 2 miles to the stop sign in Carson. Go right onto Wind River road and follow it 13 miles. Just past the Carson Fish hatchery the road forks—stay straight on Mineral Springs Road. In 1.0 mile it turns to gravel and begins the Gov't Mineral Sprgs loop. The camp and t'head are at the far end of the loop.

Drive from Portland: Take I-84 east to Cascade Locks exit 44. At the end of the exit turn right and cross the Bridge of the Gods. Turn right onto Hwy 14 and follow it 6 miles, through Stevenson, to the flashing Hwy light and signs for Carson (near MP 47.5). Turn left here onto Wind River road and go 1 mile to the 4-way stop. Go straight through the stop and pick up the above directions heading 13 miles north.

- Drivetime from Portland: 68 min
- from Hood River: 40 min
- Fee: NW Forest Pass (none nearby)
- Restroom: yes

HIKE: Begin both hikes at the campground. Head right, pass Iron Mike spring, and come to the orange 'Road Closed' gate. Go around the gate and walk .25 miles, passing cabins on your right. When the road starts uphill fork right onto the trail. At the sign-in box fill out a free wilderness pass then continue .5 miles to a creek crossing. After rock-hopping across the creek you come to a junction with the Soda Peaks Lake Trail 133. **Go left here for a difficult 4.0 mile climb to the lake, returning the way you came.**

For the easier outing, go right to begin a 2.5 mile loop. In .3 miles you'll come to the falling-down bridge over Trapper Creek. Carefully cross the bridge and look for the trail sign—this is where the loop part starts and ends. Head left on Soda Peaks Trail to climb .2 miles to the junction with Trapper Creek Trail 192. Go right, cross the bridge, and hike an easy canyon trail for 1.0 miles to a 4-way junction. Go right and you'll quickly find the road. Go right on the road (passing by more quaint cabins) for about .75 miles, cross the small feeder creek and back to the Trapper Creek bridge. From here retrace your steps 0.75 miles back to the campground.

Tree hugging an 8-foot+ Douglas fir

Scenic Hike/Waterfall

15

Roundtrip time-guess from Portland: 4.5 or 6 hours
from Hood River: 3.5 or 5 hours

Difficulty level: easy 2-mile one-way <u>or</u> diff 5-mile loop
Highlights: ★★★★★ Waterfall and old-growth

Falls Creek Falls Trails

As Meatloaf said, "Two out of three ain't bad"

For waterfall lovers this one is a must-see...you ***will*** say "Wow"! This astonishing three-tiered masterpiece awaits at the end of a beautiful 2.0 mile trail. The trail follows Falls Creek upstream through groves of old-growth before ending at the base of this 250-foot waterfall—impressive! But, as great as this viewpoint is, you can only see two of the three tiers. To see the upper tier you have two challenging options. The **First Option** is to scramble up the steep trail that leads to the top of the middle tier. This vantage is awesome—from here you see the upper cascade as well as a birds-eye peek down over the lower falls.

The **Second Option** hooks you up with the Upper Falls Trail to complete a 5-mile loop back to your car. It's an extreme, root grappling, ladder-like gully climb to the very top of the falls! Sadly, at the top you can hear the falls you've just conquered but the view is obscured. **This option is rugged and dangerous**—the only reason to do it is to make the loop. If you've got competent scrambling skills, it's a fun climb.

An "extreme" hiker loving the root gully.

DRIVING: **From Hood River:** Cross theHR bridge and go left on Hwy 14 for 15.5 miles. Just past the Wind River bridge (near MP 50) turn right onto Hot Springs Avenue. Go 2.0 miles to the stop sign in Carson. Go right onto Wind River road and follow it 13.0 miles. Just past the Carson Fish hatchery the road forks—stay right on Wind River road. In another .8 miles look for the gravel Forest Road 3062 sign and turn right. Follow signs for Upper Falls Creek Falls Trail. There are a number of roads branching off this one but you want to stay straight to the end, to Upper Falls Trailhead 152.

From Portland: Take I-84 east to Cascade Locks exit 44. At the end of the exit turn right and cross the Bridge of the Gods. Turn right onto Hwy 14 and follow it 6 miles, through Stevenson, to the flashing Hwy light and signs for Carson (near MP 47.5). Turn left here onto Wind River road and go 1 mile to the 4-way stop. Go straight through the stop and pick up the above directions heading 13 miles north.

- **Drivetime from Portland: 70 min**
- **from Hood River: 43 min**
- **Fee: NW Forest Pass (none nearby)**
- **Restroom: no**

HIKE: Start on Trail 152 from the parking area signboard. It quickly branches. The left branch, going over the bridge, is Upper Falls Trail (the return trail on Option 2). For now stay to the right of the creek and take the narrow trail. In .5 miles it joins trail 152A– Lower Falls Viewpoint Trail. (**Take special note here,** *you return via this unsigned junction on the easy O/B hikes...don't miss it or you get to the wrong trailhead.*) Head left on trail 152A. The next 0.75 miles are easy, then the trail steepens for the final .75 miles to the waterfall. This is the endpoint of the easy trail. The less fit or confident should turn around here.

Rugged waterfall lovers continue up for **Option 1**. Find the scramble trail that begins by the big rocks. This is a supersteep hands-and-feet scramble for sure-footed people only. This 'trail' levels out as it reaches the height of the middle tier. Before getting to the falls, notice the steep, washed-out gully (it has big, exposed roots on the left side) that you carefully pick your way past. This gully is the 'extreme' loop route. After enjoying the middle tier area either retrace the trail down, or…

Begin **Option 2 up the gully.** The first 15 feet sum up the difficulty of the whole 75-foot climb. If you are gung-ho, up the gully you go. There are plenty of exposed roots that you must use to pull yourself up. Difficult yes, but the whole 75-foot climb has solid handholds. Whew! When you make it to the top of the falls the scramble continues up and left to a flat perch overlooking the forested valley.

To complete the loop take the faint trail from the perch back into the forest. In about 50 yards it meets the unsigned Upper Falls Trail 152. Go left here…but, in about .25 miles, there is a faint path cutting left that leads to a view of the upper falls After 2.3 miles the trail levels out. Look for the first trail branching to the left. Take this unsigned trail, quickly crossing the bridge and back to the parking area (if you miss the fork, you come to a wide creek—go back). What a great loop, eh!

Exploration/Waterfall

16

Roundtrip time-guess from Portland: 3 hours
from Hood River: 2 hours

Difficulty level: easy viewpoint or difficult scramble to base
Highlights: ★★★★★ amazingly lush waterfall

Panther Creek Falls

A true off-the-beaten-path **five-star spectacle**! While the throngs flock to Multnomah, only cascade connoisseurs find their way to Panther Creek Falls. Though hidden in the hills above Carson, a paved forest road goes right by the 150-yard path to the falls. This waterfall features two separate creeks tumbling about 80 feet, side-by-side. One is a beautiful curtain of water split by fingers of moss, the other a roaring slot. Hidden downstream 200 feet the creeks join and pour over another 30-foot ledge. Explore the lower canyon to see the whole 5-star moss-a-riffic package!

New view platform built in '04

EXPLORE: From the parking area backtrack on the road a little and look for a trail cutting into the trees. The trail leads to the top viewpoint. Left of the viewpoint, under a downed tree is a scramble path that leads to the super-mossy lower level. This difficult scramble path involves one rock-climbing move and lots of steep slipperiness. From the bottom curious folk can scramble down further to the area beneath the lower falls.

DRIVING: **From Hood River:** Cross the HR bridge and go left on Hwy 14 for 15.5 miles. Just past the Wind River bridge (near MP 50) turn right onto Hot Springs avenue. Go 2.0 miles to the stop sign in Carson. Turn right onto Wind River road and drive 4.7 miles to Old State road (Pass the first Old State road junction—you want the second one by the Panther Creek campground sign.). Turn right onto Old State road, then immediately left onto Panther Creek road. **Set your odometer here!** Follow this paved road for 7.2 uphill, twisting miles. After 4.0 miles you cross the Panther Creek bridge. Keep going another 3.2 miles, you're looking for a large dirt pullout on the right side of the road. It's the only large pullout in the area and it has a basalt hill towering over it. (There's a small bridge just past the pullout, if you cross this you've gone too far.)
From Portland: Take I-84 east to Cascade Locks exit 44. At the end of the exit turn right and cross the bridge. Turn right onto Hwy 14 and follow it 6 miles, through Stevenson, to the flashing Hwy light and signs for Carson (near MP 47.5). Turn left here onto Wind River road and go 1 mile to the 4-way stop. Go straight through the stop and pick up the above directions heading 4.7 miles north.

- **Drivetime from Portland: 68 min**
- **from Hood River: 40 min**
- **Fee: free**
- **Restroom: no**

A moss kingdom at the lower level

Scenic Hike/Columbia and Mountain Views

17

Roundtrip time-guess from Portland: 4 hours
from Hood River: 2.75 hours

Difficulty level: mod/diff 1.75-mile one way
Highlights: Deep forest trail, amazing summit views

Wind Mountain Trail

Wind Mountain is the distinctive cone-shaped peak (the magma chamber of an extinct volcano) that rises 1,907 feet above the Columbia near Home Valley. A lightly used but well-made 1.75 mile moderate/difficult trail leads through deep forest to a glorious 360° view at the apex. The whole western Gorge past Beacon Rock to Crown Point is visible. Mt. St. Helens and Mt. Adams are in the distance while Dog Mountain, Mt. Defiance, and Table Mountain surround you. The summit also has a Native American cultural site with an interpretive sign that explains some fascinating history.

Try this overlooked trail, it gets few visitors because it is not signed or publicized. Because the parking area is at a 700-foot elevation, the trail only rises 1,200 feet to the summit (compared to Dog Mountain's 2,800-foot rise). Less punishment for a similarly excellent view.

Wow, watching a storm blow in over Beacon Rock

DRIVING: **From Hood River:** Cross HR bridge and go left on Hwy 14 for 14.5 miles. Just past milepost 51 turn right on Wind Mtn road and follow this 1.3 miles. Turn right onto Girl Scout road and go .2 miles. Park where the pavement ends at the flat gravel area.

From Portland: Take I-84 east to Cascade Locks. At the end of the exit turn right and cross the bridge. Go right on Hwy 14 for 11 miles, passing Stevenson and on to Home Valley. Just past the mini-mart, at MP 50.5, turn left onto Wind Mtn road. Go 1.3 miles then right on Girl Scout to parking.

- **Drivetime from Portland: 53 min**
- **from Hood River: 20 min**
- **Fee: free**
- **Restroom: no**

Mt. St. Helens from the summit
(was 9,677 ft., reduced to 8,365 ft. on 5/18/80)

HIKE: The straightforward trail to the top has no options. Leave the parking area and head down the dirt road about 200 yards to find the unmarked trail on the right. After about 0.5 miles a spur trail leads left and steeply down to a pretty cool rock outcropping. After checking this out, continue on to the top.

Interpretive sign near the summit

Scenic Hike/Wildflowers/Columbia and Mtn Views

18

Roundtrip time-guess from Portland: 6 hours
from Hood River: 4 hours

Difficulty level: difficult 7-mile loop
Highlights: Sweet views, epic late-May wildflowers

Dog Mountain Trail

This super popular 2,948-foot mountain is renown for its commanding views as well as a dazzling wildflower display on the summit slope. The three difficult trails to the peak are all between 3 and 4 miles. Despite their difficulty, these trails are very popular throughout the spring and summer.

The panorama from the summit is unquestionably Gorgeous and the trailhead is easy to find. But, for some people, the unrelenting pitch, the aching knees, and the crowds on these hikes make them wonder if there exists a descriptive, easy-to-use guidebook that lists other hiking options. Oh well, too bad, you're stuck with *Curious Gorge*...ha!

But really, the best time to hike this trail is when the wildflower-a-rama explodes—usually the last two weeks of May. But beware the crowds...there can be upwards of 150 cars jamming the lot on May weekends—distastefully California-esque! For a less tortuous viewpoint hike you could try Hamilton Mtn (entry 12), Wind Mtn (entry 17), or Indian Point (entry 24).

The eastern view from the Scenic trail

DRIVING: **From Hood River:** Cross HR bridge and go left on Hwy 14 for 11.3 miles. Just past milepost 54, turn into the signed parking area. **From Portland:** Take I-84 east to Cascade Locks exit 44. At the end of the exit turn right and cross the bridge. Go right on Hwy 14 for 12 miles, passing Stevenson and Home Valley, until you get to the signed pulloff at MP 53.5.

- **Drivetime from Portland: 56 min**
- **from Hood River: 15 min**
- **Fee: NW Forest Pass (@ T'head)**
- **Restroom: yes**

Geez, 150+ cars in May 2002

HIKE: There are three trails to the summit. The steepest is the Old trail, a 3.1 mile chore. More moderate is the Scenic trail, a 3.5 mile trail that branches off the Old trail then rejoins it near the top. The best trail is the Augspurger Mtn trail, a very scenic and less steep 3.7 mile option. The best hike is probably looping together the Scenic trail and the Augspurger Mtn trail. Some people prefer to climb steeply and come down gently. Other people prefer the opposite—you pick.

To climb the Scenic Trail, begin by reading the map at the trailhead. Start to the right of the parking area, soon passing the restrooms. Climb steeply to the trail junction with the Old trail. Stay right, as marked, for the less difficult Scenic trail. Through the woods and past a vista you eventually rejoin the Old trail to the peak. At the remnant of the old fire lookout the trail splits. The right fork is easier but has no view. The left fork traverses the wildflower slope. Chose either, they rejoin just under the peak. Once at the summit, after a well-deserved rest, head back down the summit trail to meet the Augspurger trail. Go right, cross the face, then descend into the forest on the northwest side of the mountain. Stay left at the only junction and in an hour you'll be back at your car.

The summit view over Wind Mountain

Exploration/Waterfalls

19

Roundtrip time-guess from Portland: 3.5 hours
from Hood River: 2 hours

Difficulty level: easy view or difficult adventure
Highlights: Canyon chock-full-o-cascades

Dog Creek Falls

A waterfall adventurer's paradise! The first waterfall (of many) is the 25-foot cascade in view right off Hwy 14—a great picnic spot on a hot day. But the secret splendors of Dog Creek are the smaller waterfalls hidden further upstream. This canyon is wicked-steep, so it's like a million little waterfalls the whole way up it. To get to these picturesque rewards... you'll need to conquer some challenges. First, getting to the second tier of falls and beyond requires rock-climbing up the imposing front face. It looks hard but it's not too tough if you're athletic. This canyon begs adventure, and delivers surprise—you can scramble up, over, and around various cascades for at least an hour! How far will your curiosity take you? One time in an upper, upper waterfall there were a few guys and girls taking artistic nude photographs. Wow, bring a friend and take some yourself!!

Have a Dog Creek-style picnic right off Hwy 14

DRIVING: **From Hood River:** Cross HR bridge and go left on Hwy 14 for 9.2 miles. Past milepost 56 look for a sign reading 'Dog Creek' and pull into the large gravel parking area on the right side.
From Portland: Take I-84 east to Cascade Locks exit 44. At the end of the exit turn right and cross the bridge. Go right on Hwy 14 for 15 miles, passing Stevenson, Home Valley, and Dog Mtn until you get to the signed pulloff at MP 56.

Spawned-out salmon, fall 2001

EXPLORE: The easiest way to the second tier is straight up the rock face immediately to the left of the falls. The scree paths to the left of the face look easy but actually lead to scarier, sketchy moves. Use your head...are you sure-footed?... are you sober?? Be sure you are up to this challenge! *FYI: the climb back down the face, with your butt to the rock, isn't too hard.*

From the bottom climb up the rock face towards the little tree. At the tree, head right, check out the 2nd falls, and then work your way to the top. Past the second tier the going gets easier as you scramble and rock-hop up the faint paths to still more beautiful and private cascades. Eventually, after about an hour, you might come to an unclimbable waterfall. Who knows? Turn back whenever your curiosity abates.

Upper cascade art

Exploration/Natural Wonder

20

Roundtrip time-guess from Portland: 4.5 hours
from Hood River: 2.5 hours

Difficulty level: easy to look, difficult to explore
Highlights: Fantastic ice stalactites in spring

Ice Cave

The Ice Cave is one of the most unbelievable wonders near the Gorge—when springtime conditions are right! During winter water seeps and drips from the cave's ceiling, freezing to create a miniature Carlsbad Caverns. No limestone though, just icicles. You'll find magnificent floor-to-ceiling frozen pillars, delicate draperies of transparent ice, and stalactites and stalagmites galore. Amazingly, this cave renews itself yearly and each year's formations are different depending on rainfall, temperature, and *magic.*

The cave is interesting and worth a visit anytime, but wait too long into the summer and all the icicles melt. The earlier you visit in the spring the better. April and May are best, some years June can still be good, but by July there are only remnants of the formations. The most intricate ice is down the short entrance staircase and way back to the left. The portion of the cave to the right of the staircase is also fun to explore—it weaves over and around boulders for about 100 yards then re-emerges above ground. Check out the 'natural bridge' alcove, a neat cave feature 50 feet to the right of the staircase.

Icicles near the staircase

DRIVING: **From Hood River:** Cross HR bridge and go left on Hwy 14 for 1.5 miles. Turn right onto Alt. 141 and drive 2 miles to a stop sign junction with Hwy 141. Turn left and proceed 19 miles to Trout Lake. At the gas station stay left on 141 and drive another 6.5 miles. You'll pass the ranger station and continue straight when 141 changes to FS24. Turn left at the sign for the Ice Cave and go .25 miles to parking.

From Portland: Take I-84 to Hood River exit 64 then follow above directions.

- **Drivetime from Portland: 95 min**
- **from Hood River: 40 min**
- **Fee: free**
- **Restroom: yes**

Pam and Mike on their stalagmite throne

EXPLORE: The inside of the cave is very cold—even on a hot summer day. It's also wet and very slippery on the icy areas. Accessing the icicles requires scrambling over and around small boulders. It is dark, very dark. **Things to bring: two flashlights or a lantern, warm clothes including jacket, long pants, hat, gloves, and solid shoes.** Many people visit without knowing just how dark and chilly the cave is and have to cut short their explorations. As Mr. T would say, "I pity the fool!" Go prepared!

In April or May, first call the Gifford Pinchot Ranger Station to check road conditions. The last half-mile of road to the cave is not plowed, and impassable for most vehicles until the snow melts. Their phone is 509-395-2501. You can also drive to where the plows stop and then walk the last .5 miles of road over the snowmobile-packed snow. If you do this, turn left at the Ice Cave sign and trek .25 miles into the forest until you get to a clearing near a signboard. You'll find the 30-foot cave opening and staircase on the left side of this clearing/parking area.

NOTE: Natural Bridges and more caves are located 1.0 miles past the Ice Caves on FS24.

Gorge Attraction/Lake

21

Roundtrip time-guess from Portland: 4 hours
from Hood River: 1 hour

Difficulty level: easy
Highlights: fishing, wading, boating

Northwestern Lake Park

Northwestern Lake is the quiet reservoir behind Condit Dam on the White Salmon River. The lakeside park is a great place for family gatherings or just cooling off with your dogs or kids. Scattered amongst the pines and firs are about twenty picnic tables and barbeque grills. Fishermen love the stocked lake, so put your bass-boat in at the boat ramp or cast from the dock or shore. Rafters and kayakers use the park as their take-out point on the lower river run, so on weekends you'll see plenty of happy groups ending their river trips.

The river moves slowly enough that kids and dogs love to wade in the chilly, shallow water (grown-ups chill with a beer!). When the Gorge is really windy, this "lake" is less so…and when the Gorge is way hot, Northwestern Lake is cool.

Happy rafters

DRIVING: **From Hood River:** Cross HR bridge and go left on Hwy 14 for 1.5 miles. Turn right onto Alt. 141 and drive 2.0 miles to the stop sign. Turn left onto Hwy 141 and drive 1.9 miles to Northwestern Lake Road. Turn left down this road and in .4 miles cross the bridge to the park entrance.

From Portland: Take I-84 to Hood River exit 64 then follow above directions.

- Drivetime from Portland: 70 min
- from Hood River: 15 min
- Fee: free
- Restroom: yes

A post-rafting BBQ Beer bash

Dogs and kids frolic happily!

NOTE: Located just past the lake's entrance you'll find the Buck Creek Trail system. A signboard at the end of Northwestern Lake Road details the maze of hiking and biking trails.

Gorge Attraction/Exploration/Scenic Hike

22

Roundtrip time-guess from Portland: 3 hours
from Hood River: 1 hour

Difficulty level: easy view or easy 1-mile one-way stroll
Highlights: Controversial dam in beautiful river canyon

Condit Dam

The giant Condit Dam fills a narrow canyon on the White Salmon River, creating Northwestern Lake. Built in 1913 to provide hydroelectric power for a growing regional population, this monstrous 123-foot high dam now generates only a tiny fraction of the Bonneville Power Administration hydroelectric grid. Unfortunately, this dam blocks all upstream migration of spawning salmon. Thus, Condit Dam has become one of the crux battlegrounds in the U.S. for fish habitat restoration and obsolete dam removal. Currently an 'explosive' plan is in place to remove the dam and return the river to its natural course. For info about the dam's removal plan, Google "Condit Dam removal"—the current plan is to blow a hole in the dam in Oct. 2008.

When the White Salmon was dammed, the white salmon were damned. Regardless of this controversy, the dam is an interesting, fun place to visit.

Condit Dam water flume walkway

Imagine the White Salmon once again filled with white salmon

DRIVING: **From Hood River:** Cross HR bridge and go left on Hwy 14 for 1.5 miles. Turn right onto Alt. 141 and drive 2.0 miles to the stop sign. Turn left on 141 and go .8 miles to Powerhouse road (at the 'Leaving Scenic Area' sign). Turn left and proceed .4 miles. The unsigned, one-lane dam access road forks down and right—take this to the parking area (if you come to the house on the left by a turn, you've gone too far). Park and go around the gate to get to the dam.

- **Drivetime from Portland: 69 min**
- **from Hood River: 13 min**
- **Fee: free**
- **Restroom: no**

From Portland: Take I-84 to Hood River exit 64 then follow above directions.

HIKE: To view the face of the dam you need to descend a 5-step ladder and a short staircase found to the left of the main dam structure. The stairs bring you to a walkway on top of a large wooden pipe. This 'flume' carries pressurized water downstream to the powerhouse. Take a stroll on the 1.0 mile walkway—it's pretty unique. Feel free to explore the many ladders and scramble paths down to the river's edge.

Condit Dam waterfall

Gorge Attraction/Columbia and Mountain Views

23

Roundtrip time-guess from Portland: 2.5 hours
from Hood River: 30 minutes

Difficulty level: easy drive-up views
Highlights: Panoramic vista of Hood River Valley & Columbia

Cook-Underwood Road Viewpoint

Check out this inspiring drive-to viewpoint on Cook-Underwood road! The expansive panorama is enough to make anyone stop their car to gape—fortunately two large gravel pullouts are provided.

From this 1,000-foot bluff the Columbia stretches past the Hood River bridge towards Mosier and McCall Point. All of the Hood River valley, from Mt. Hood to downtown, unfolds before you. On windy summer days look directly down on the Spring Creek Hatchery and watch the hordes of windsurfers jumping and jibing as if you were in a helicopter. The Columbia Gorge Hotel and its resident waterfall, Wah Gwin Gwin, are directly across the river.

Catch a sunset at this wonderful place and ponder our curious Gorge... imagine the Columbia filled with water to this very point during the Missoula Floods 10,000 to 15,000 years ago. Whoa!

The kiting sandbar, the Event site, and even Mosier

DRIVING: **From Hood River:** Cross HR bridge and go left on Hwy 14 for 1.5 miles. After crossing the White Salmon bridge turn right on Cook-Underwood road. Drive 3.0 miles to the two large gravel pullouts on the left side.

- **Drivetime from Portland: 65 min**
- **from Hood River: 10 min**
- **Fee: free**
- **Restroom: no**

From Portland: Take I-84 to Hood River exit 64 then follow above directions.

From Hatchery to Hood

Scenic Hike/Columbia and Mountain Views

24

Roundtrip time-guess from Portland: 5.5 hours
from Hood River: 4.5 hours

Difficulty level: Difficult 4 miles one-way
Highlights: Unique outcropping and outstanding views

Indian Point Trail

This 4.0 mile trail is a sustained but moderate uphill hike to a uniquely recognizable rock outcropping. Indian Point, at 2,600 feet, is like a basalt thumb that protrudes from Nick Eaton Ridge across the river from Wind Mountain. Once you've been to this outcropping you'll always look for it as you cross the Hood River bridge or when driving west along the Columbia—the point is surprisingly prominent!

The trail surface is immaculate—the author saw two people walk it barefoot! Once you work your way down to the point, bravehearts can scramble left around the knob to the very edge. Careful though, it's a 1,000-foot drop straight down! St. Helens and Adams are in their glory while Wind Mountain looks tiny. Check out the whole Gorge to Hood River. It's easy to spend an hour here resting, eating, and identifying all the curious Gorge landmarks!

Overall, the hike itself isn't too exciting—no views or creeks—but the viewpoint itself is super worth the effort! Don't climb Dog Mountain again until you try this hike.

The thumb-like Indian Point

DRIVING: **From Hood River:** Take I-84 west to Herman Creek exit 47. Go left under the hwy, then right towards Oxbow hatchery. In .5 miles turn left into Herman Creek campground. Follow the road up then right to the trailhead parking area.

From Portland: Take I-84 east to Cascade Locks exit 44. Go straight 1.5 miles through town, cross over I-84, and continue on the frontage road another 1.7 miles to Herman Creek camp. Turn right, up the road then right to the trailhead.

- **Drivetime from Portland: 45 min**
- **from Hood River: 18 min**
- **Fee: NW Forest Pass (in campground)**
- **Restroom: yes**

The view from I-84

HIKE: Start at the 'Herman Creek and PCT ¼ mile' trail sign (this info is wrong). Start steeply up and in .25 miles intersect with the powerline road. Go up and right and the trail resumes .4 miles to the PCT junction. To reach Indian Point stay left on the Herman Creek Trail which widens to a road as it climbs .7 miles to the trail-camp junction. **Careful here.** Go left on the intersecting road and look for the 'Gorton Creek Trail/ Ridge Cutoff, 2.6 miles' sign.

Note: The Herman Creek Trail goes straight, passing the Nick Eaton Ridge Trail, to Wahtum Lake. The trail to the left of the sign is Gorge Trail 400 to Wyeth.

Head up the Gorton Creek Trail for 2.6 miles until it finally switchbacks up to the Ridge Cutoff trail. (Note: you can make a loop on the way back by taking this Cutoff .5 miles up and then right onto Nick Eaton trail for a super-steep 2.5 mile descent…but this is for loop-fiends only—it's too arduous for most folks' tired legs.) To continue to Indian Point, pass the Ridge Cutoff 100 feet and look left for the unsigned spur trail that leads steeply down 200 yards to the point.

After your rest and relaxation either retrace your steps or suffer the loop option. On the way back you can cut .3 miles down to Herman Creek for a nice splash if you want to.

Wind and Dog Mountain to the east of Indian Point

Exploration/Waterfall

25

Roundtrip time-guess from Portland: 2.5 hours
from Hood River: 1.5 hours

Difficulty level: moderate .75 miles one-way
Highlights: Boulder-hopping creekbed scramble

Gorton Creek Falls

A captivating 80-foot cascade is the reward for this 0.75 mile hike-n-scramble up the Gorton creekbed from Wyeth Campground. It's curious to note that there is no mention of this waterfall on any of the campground signage...only in the Gorge do 80-foot falls remain "secret"—anywhere else these falls would be a "highlight"!

The creekbed is a pretty one with all its moss and little waterfalls and it's a fun challenge to go up it. The basalt amphitheater around the base of the waterfall is a peaceful place to escape the Gorge winds, have a snack and a beer, and maybe get your girlfriend to pose for "arty" shot on the rock in front of the falls.

Christina and Scott on a photo adventure

DRIVING: **From Hood River:** Take I-84 west to Wyeth exit 51. Go left under the hwy then right on Herman Creek road. In 200 yards turn left into Wyeth campground. Follow trailhead signs straight back to the parking area.

- **Drivetime from Portland: 45 min**
- **from Hood River: 15 min**
- **Fee: NW Forest Pass (at camp host)**
- **Restroom: yes**

From Portland: Take I-84 east to Wyeth exit 51. Go right, then right again, and then left into campground. T'head is all the way back.

Hop up this creekbed to the waterfall

NOTE: During wet conditions the scramble up the creekbed is possible but can be very slippery and tricky. It's better to plan for wet feet (sandals or old shoes) than it is to take too many risks trying to hop from one wet mossy rock to another.

EXPLORE: From the parking area head into the forest past the signboard (the falls are not shown on the sign). The trail is a double track until you reach a signed trail junction. Go straight past the sign. The trail ends at the rock—take to the creek itself. Now you have to rockhop the final 200 yards to the base of the waterfall. The right side of the creek is easier at first, then cross and finish on the left side.

Exploration/Columbia Views

26

Roundtrip time-guess from Portland: 2.25 hours
from Hood River: 1.25 hours

Difficulty level: easy-ish .5-mile one-way
Highlights: Historic site

Shellrock Mountain 1872 Wagon Road

Explore this little remnant of Gorge history before Mother Nature reclaims it! In a quarter-mile you'll journey back over 100 years of road-making history. Park alongside our modern interstate highway (completed in 1956), walk over the Historic Columbia River Highway (built around 1916), and then pick your way up to the Wagon Road (circa 1872)—neat! The Wagon Road was one of the first roadbuilding attempts in the Gorge. Surprisingly, portions of this road survive on the talus slopes of Shellrock Mountain, resembling a castle wall in places with a surface covered in thick springy moss.

Walking the .4-mile remnant of the road, you can't help but reflect on the difficulty involved in establishing the first roads amidst all the unyielding basalt, talus slopes, and canyons of the Gorge.

Astoundingly intact sections of dry masonry

DRIVING: **From Hood River:** The trailhead is only accessible from I-84 eastbound. Take I-84 west to Wyeth exit 51. Go left under the bridge then get back on I-84 east. In 1.0 miles you'll see a high metal retaining wall on your right. Slow down and prepare to pull off onto the shoulder just past the end of the two retaining walls. Drive to the far end of the pulloff and park where the guardrail begins. Look for the Dept of Trans sign behind the guardrail.
From Portland: Take I-84 east towards exit 51 and follow above directions.

- Drivetime from Portland: 45 min
- from Hood River: 14 min
- Fee: free
- Restroom: no

Looking across the river to Wind Mountain

EXPLORE: From the highway shoulder climb over the guardrail and begin walking east through the trees. This is the surface of the Historic Highway. In about 150 yards look for a path on your right where the rocky slope begins. Scramble up onto this path and follow it as it switchbacks up to the wagon road. Looking up you can see the wall of the road. Once up to the mossy roadbed you can explore both left into the trees and right to some other intact sections.

At the left end of the road a path heads up Shellrock's talus slope. This path eventually leads to an overgrown fire lookout station. The trail is in terrible shape, covered by lots of downed trees and brush. Don't bother with this extension—it's not worth it.

Exploration/Waterfall

27

Roundtrip time-guess from Portland: 2.5 hours
from Hood River: 1 hour

Difficulty level: easy walk to view area
Highlights: Big waterfall right off highway

Starvation Creek Falls

Starvation Creek Falls is an impressive 190-foot, two-tiered cataract. Somehow this waterfall remains lightly visited even though the viewing/picnic table area is directly off I-84 and the paved path to the falls is only 100 yards long. Maybe people coming from the west are already waterfalled-out by the time they get this far...yay, no crowd.

Starvehenge view

There are a couple of creekside picnic tables at the falls that invite lingering...but if you want a more enchanting spot you can scramble up the creek, cross it once or twice and climb up onto the boulder. This "secret" spot atop the boulder has an array of strange "starve-henge" blocks created by some mysterious Historic Hwy druids—good seats to really see the magnificence of the whole waterfall. Hmmm, what purpose did these micro-monoliths serve??

DRIVING: **From Hood River:** The parking is only accessible from I-84 eastbound. Take I-84 west to Wyeth exit 51. Go left under the bridge then get back on I-84 east. Drive 4 miles back to Starvation Creek exit 55.

- **Drivetime from Portland: 48 min**
- **from Hood River: 17 min**
- **Fee: free**
- **Restroom: yes**

From Portland: Take I-84 east to Starvation Falls exit 55.

EXPLORE: If you're adventurous and surefooted you can try to find the 'secret' ridgetop waterfall vista. From this ridge you get a killer view of the whole 190-foot falls, plus a view down the Columbia... as well as complete solitude. To get there follow the paved path over the bridge towards Viento Park. 100 feet past the bridge there's an old aluminum pipe that leads up the steep hillside. Following the pipe, scramble up this tricky, loose, steep slope to the tank. (It is easiest to start about 100 feet past the pipe and angle your way back to it). At the water tank scramble up and right another 40 feet to the ridge. Sweet! It's a difficult but short climb to the 'secret spot'; it only takes 5 to 10 minutes and the birdseye view is awesome!

Ridge top view of Starvation Creek Falls

Scenic Hike/Waterfalls/Columbia Views

28

Roundtrip time-guess from Portland: 3.25 hours
from Hood River: 2 hours

Difficulty level: moderate 2.5-mile loop
Highlights: Four closely clustered waterfalls

Starvation Ridge Waterfalls Trail

This moderate 2.5 mile loop packs in plenty of sights plus a decent workout for its short length. Highway noise is bothersome at first but the effect fades as you go. The hike features a very steep .5 mile climb (or a steep descent if you prefer to do the loop in reverse), a terrific cliff-edge Columbia/Dog Mountain viewpoint, a rock-hop across both Cabin Creek and Warren Creek, and to top it off, three different waterfalls in the final .75 miles of trail. Whew!

These three falls plus the one at Starvation Creek (east of the parking area) are the most closely clustered waterfalls in the eastern half of the Gorge.

Cabin Creek Falls . . . super photo friendly!

DRIVING: **From Hood River:** The parking is only accessible from I-84 eastbound. Take I-84 west to Wyeth exit 51. Go left under the bridge then get back on I-84 east. Drive 4 miles back to Starvation Creek exit 55.

From Portland: Take I-84 east to Starvation Falls exit 55.

- **Drivetime from Portland: 48 min**
- **from Hood River: 17 min**
- **Fee: free**
- **Restroom: yes**

HIKE: From the parking area head west .25 miles on the paved path next to the hwy and turn left onto the Starvation Cutoff trail at the signed junction. The next .5 miles are super-super-steep switchbacks. At the unsigned Starvation Ridge trail go right. From here it's 1.0 miles to the Mt. Defiance Trail junction. This up and down trail crosses Cabin Creek and then climbs to a cliff-edge viewpoint. After a stop, descend to Warren Creek and further to the Mt. Defiance trail. Turning right here completes the loop, but first go left and walk 100 yards to see Lancaster Falls (named after Samuel Lancaster, designer of the Historic Columbia River Highway). *This trail continues another grueling 4,500 vertical feet to the top of Mt. Defiance, but for this hike turn around and head back down .75 miles towards the hwy.* At Warren Creek scramble for an up-close view of Tunnel Falls (Historic Hwy engineers diverted the creek from its original falls through this tunnel in order to keep the hwy dry). After the bridge, if you're curious, you can go up the dry creekbed to see the original waterfall basin.

The base of Tunnel Falls

Continue east back to the noisy hwy and look for pretty Cabin Creek Falls (partially hidden behind a big boulder). Finally, walk past the cutoff trail back to your car.

Lancaster Falls

Scenic Hike/Columbia Views

29

Roundtrip time-guess from Portland: 3 hours
from Hood River: 1.5 hours
Difficulty level: mod/diff 1.3 miles one-way
Highlights: Poetic Columbia views

Mitchell Point Trail

This gem of a trail is one of the Gorge's many quirky curiosities—there is no signage indicating that this excellent trail even exists! But yes, a steep mod/diff trail climbs 1.3 miles to the jutting, knife-edge ridge called Mitchell Point. From this 1,200-foot ridge the view is superb. To the west the Columbia weaves sinuously between Dog Mountain and Indian Point...ahhh,this view of the river winding through the heart of the Gorge is !!!!!! (featured in a great poster by ace photographer Peter Marbach). Across the river look for remnants of the Broughton Flume on the hillside above Drano Lake. To the east you'll see past the 'The Hatchery' (the windsurfing mecca) all the way to the Hood River bridge. Impressive!

Approaching Li'l & Big Mitchell on I-84

DRIVING: **From Hood River:** The trailhead is only accessible from I-84 eastbound. Take I-84 west to Viento exit 56. Return on I-84 east to Mitchell Point exit 58.
From Portland: Take I-84 east to exit 58.

- Drivetime from Portland: 51 min
- from Hood River: 9 min
- Fee: free
- Restroom: yes

This hike can either be a quick, lung-pumping workout or a leisurely climb to a spot worth hanging out at for an hour. Many pages of this book were actually scripted and edited while atop this ridge...the view definitely helps inspire exclamation marks!

The skinny, exposed rock ridge at the top may not be suitable for dogs, kids, or those who fear heights, but there are also great viewpoints before the ridge-end that are less exposed. If you want something quick and Gorge-ous near Hood River, try this one!

Soooo beautiful!!

HIKE: **Note 1:Before hiking check out the interpretive sign overlooking the hwy.**
Note 2: Be careful of poison oak near the top in the cleared/brushy area under the powerlines.

From the parking area head up the paved path past the 'Lausmann' sign. As this path turns toward a plaque, an unsigned trail branches left and heads uphill. Take this trail into the trees, staying left. (As you begin the climb, note how the trail is wide like on old road. This graded section is actually part of the 1872 wagon road (entry 26). Extra horse teams would laboriously haul the wagons up this hill and then through the saddle that separates the Mitchell's two humps—wow. When the trail narrows, sharp eyes can look down and see the old road grade heading towards the saddle).

Now switchback up the next 1.0 miles over forested and scree slopes. When you come out at a saddle under the powerlines, go left and clamber the final 200 yards to the exposed ridge. Obviously, be careful. Return the way you came.

Scenic Hike/Columbia Views

30

Roundtrip time-guess from Portland: 3 or 4.5 hours
from Hood River: 1.5 or 3 hours

Difficulty level: easy 1.5-mile one-way or mod 6-mile loop
Highlights: Viewpoints, deep forest, creeks

Wygant / Chetwoot Trails

These two trails, along with the Mitchell Point trail, are the closest deep-forest trails to Hood River. Your first option here is an easy, family-friendly jaunt along the first 1.5 miles of the Wygant Trail. This trail features sections of the Historic Columbia River Highway, a log-bridge crossing at Perham Creek, and at the end a spacious grassy picnic area viewpoint looking 300 feet down to the Columbia. A great Gorge sampler for people who don't hike often.

The second hike option is a 6.0 mile loop. It includes all of option one plus an additional foray on the Chetwoot Trail into the upper regions of Perham Creek. This upper loop features deep lush forest, a rock-hop across pretty Perham Creek, and a glorious upper viewpoint...Whoa, this 1,400-foot perch is sweet! Sitting amongst the June wildflower dazzle, your view spans from Stevenson to White Salmon with a peek at Mt. Adams. A wonderfully secluded spot to sit and ponder the beauties of the Gorge...*ahhh, daydream how the river's curves mimic those of Elle McPherson... mmmmm curves and conical tetons!*

The author pondering the Curious Gorge

DRIVING:

From Hood River: The trailhead is only accessible from I-84 eastbound. Take I-84 west to Viento exit 56. Return on I-84 east to Mitchell Point exit 58.

From Portland: Take I-84 east to exit 58.

Lisa crosses Perham Creek

HIKE: **Note: Be careful of poison oak on the Chetwoot when it crosses under the powerlines twice. (Sorry Chrissy!)**

Both trails start together. From Mitchell Point walk back west on the road and look for the Wygant Trail sign. The trail starts here on this section of the Historic Hwy. Follow the roadway until it bends left and becomes dirt. Now go right onto the signed singletrack trail. In the next .5 miles you'll cross Mitchell Creek then rejoin the Historic Hwy. Look for the trail sign branching off to the left and begin a .5 mile climb to the Chetwoot Trail junction—100 feet before the Perham Creek bridge/Viewpoint sign.

For the easy **Option 1** trail, head left down to the bridge. Go over the bridge and an easy .3 miles to the viewpoint picnic area—this hike's endpoint. Retrace your steps back to the car.

For **Option 2**, the longer loop, don't go down to the bridge…instead, backtrack from the Perham Creek sign 100 feet and begin the Chetwoot Loop. In .25 miles you meet the powerline service road/trail. Go right for **35 steps** and look left for the unsigned continuation of the Chetwoot Trail. The trail rises into a lush forest while the highway noise is replaced by the gurgle of Perham Creek—nice! After climbing a mile you'll get to hop across the creek. The next .5 miles are fairly level, and after a sharp left corner look for the Wygant trail branching off to the left. Go left here and switchback .5 miles to the viewpoint (the trail continues upwards another mile, but there's no better viewpoint than this one).

After a break, retrace your steps back down to the junction. Now turn left and begin a gradual 1.0 mile descent towards the lower picnic viewpoint. Pass a spur trail to another perch and some mysteriously useless guardrails, finally emerging from the forest next to the silly signpost. This area is the endpoint of the easy Wygant Trail option. From here go left past the signpost and back into the forest. The next .5 miles crosses the bridge and then climbs back to Chetwoot. Now retrace your steps to Mitchell.

Museum

31

Roundtrip time-guess from Portland: 3 hours
from Hood River: 1 hour

Difficulty level: easy
Highlights: Exhibits, videos, photos...perspective!

Hood River Museum

The Hood River Museum is a fun place to spend an hour or two—pick a rainy day, a rest day, or an early summer morning. You'll love wandering through this curious collection of Hood River memorabilia!

Colorful fruit labels

The displays of Indian beadwork are the finest around. The colorful sample of old-time fruit labels is dazzling. The painting of the Koberg Beach dance pavilion harkens back to an uncomplicated era. Kids love the life-like schoolroom, dentist office, and kitchen dioramas.

Old photo of people riding the flume

Wow, bet you've never seen better photos of people actually riding the Broughton flume! And check out the ancient windsurf gear—it'll evoke laughs and sweet memories of learning this gear-riffic sport.

- **Drivetime from Portland: 57 min**
- **from Hood River: 1 min**
- **Fee: donations accepted**
- **Restroom: yes**
- **Open: April-ish to October-ish Mon-Sat 10-4pm, Sun 12-4pm**
- **Phone: 541-386-6772**

DRIVING: **From Hood River:** Head towards HR bridge. At the 4-way intersection just before the bridge turn left. Follow signs to the museum.

From Portland: Take I-84 to Hood River exit 64 then follow above directions.

There are also videos to watch and classic books to peruse, but maybe the funnest area is the album table located upstairs. These albums contain classic newspaper clippings… the dawn of the 80's windsurf era…quaint Mt. Hood Meadows ads… businesses long forgotten…late 70's disco Hood River…. sweet stuff that'll make you laugh!

Everyone should visit for at least an hour. Come with friends, you'll all have fun—there's way more interesting stuff inside than you'd imagine from the looks of the drab outsides.

Old-time dental office

PANORAMA '84, Hood River, Oregon, Wednesday, April 25, 1984

Sailboarding in gorge now a big hit

Headlines in 1984!

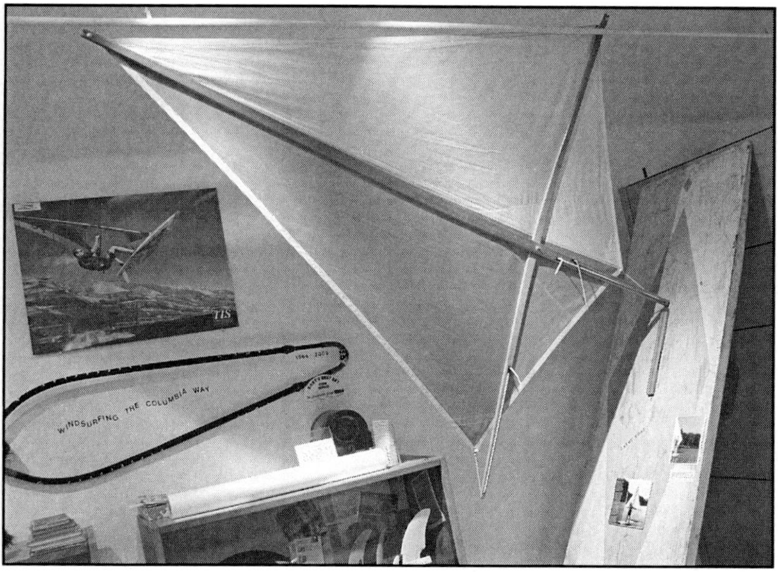

The 1964 "Darby" wind board

Scenic Hike/Unique Phenomenon

32

Roundtrip time-guess from Portland: 3 hours
from Hood River: 1 hour

Difficulty level: .75 mile one-way
Highlights: Walk atop pipe to rainbow-rama

Hood River's Rainbow Garden

If you want a hike that's out-of-the-ordinary, try this .75-mile jaunt along the top of a huge pipe, beside a beautiful river, which leads to a quirky spectacle—all just moments from downtown Hood River.

The "Rainbow Garden" is the author's pet name for a sight that is part man-made wonder and part natural wonder. The scene is this…there exists a small dam on the Hood River about 3 miles upstream from the power plant. This dam funnels water into a large 10-foot diameter pipe that pressurizes the water as it flows to the power plant. The intrigue is that, along the way, the pipe has sprung leaks and pressurized water blasts out everywhere for about a 100-yard span. The sight of the water squirting all over is neat enough—the man-made attraction part…but way better is seeing it on a sunny day between 11am and 3pm when

Who laid this pipe?

DRIVING: **From Hood River:** In HR at the 4-way stop on Hwy 35, head south on Hwy for only .2 miles. At an unmarked road quickly turn right and down over 7 bumps to the Pacific Power parking area.

- **Drivetime from Portland: 57 min**
- **from Hood River: 2 min**
- **Fee: free**
- **Restroom: yes**

From Portland: Take I-84 to Hood River exit 64, turn right and go up hill to 4-way stopsign, and follow above directions.

ZOW, Rainbows Galore!! Intense colors…huge arcs, small arcs. Hypervisible double rainbows, Megaspray ultra arcs, ROY G. BIV city! As you stroll along the pipe the rainbows all change depending on your angle to the spray—it's just magnificent!

But wait…this water and power are being "wasted", so every few years the pipe is "repaired". But then, over time, it seems to unrepair itself and begin blasting out again—¡que bueno! In fall 2001 the pipe was fixed, no more rainbows. By 2003 the 'bows were back in town, bigger than ever. Fall 2005 the pipe had been fixed again, so no 'bows…go see it in 2006… who knows when the 'bows will reign again?

Rainbows don't show in B & W

HIKE: This walk is unusual. You either can walk the .75 miles upstream on the Mt. Hood Scenic Railroad tracks, or atop the flume pipe itself. Walking the pipe is really easy and fun—try it out at the parking lot to check your balance, because upstream the pipe doesn't let you off easily until it ends. So...upstream you go. At the end of the pipe keep going and cross the bridge. Just beyond is the Rainbow Garden—if there's no spray look for the denuded areas where the water used to squirt. The flume is walkable another 2 miles to the dam, but it gets trickier, especially the dismount near the dam.

Past the rainbows along the Hood

Scenic Hike/Columbia Views

33

Roundtrip time-guess from Portland: 3-4 hours
from Hood River: 1 hour

Difficulty level: easy 4.6 miles one-way
Highlights: Paved multi-use trail

Historic Columbia River Highway Trail

Viewpoint east of Tunnels

This gloriously scenic and enchanting stretch of Sam Lancaster's original Columbia River Highway is just a few minutes drive from downtown Hood River. A 4.6-mile paved 'trail' starts in mossy, green Hood River, winds gently along basalt bluffs above the Columbia, goes through the famed Mosier Twin Tunnels, and ends in the much drier climatic zone of Mosier.

Because this trail is closed to motorized vehicles it makes a **perfect hiking, running, or dog-walking path**. It's also the best place for a family bike ride, roller-blade, or stroll near downtown. There is parking and access at both ends of the trail, but only the Hood River side has a visitor center featuring classic photos and info about the Historic Highway.

DRIVING: **From Hood River:**
Hood River Trailhead, start at the Hwy 35 4-way stop and go east on Old Columbia River Drive 1.2 miles to the parking area. ***Or*, Mosier Trailhead**, take I-84 east to Mosier exit 69. Atop the ramp turn right. As the road bends left, take your first left onto Rock Creek Road. The parking area is .8 miles up this road, just past the trailhead entrance by 50 yards.

From Portland: Take I-84 to Hood River exit 64. Turn right and go up hill to the 4-way stop. Turn left and climb 1.2 miles to the parking lot.

- **Drivetime from Portland: 60 min**
- **from Hood River: 4 min**
- **Fee: $3 state park @ trailhead**
- **Restroom: yes**

Kate and the twin mounds of Inspiration Point

HIKE: The popular twin tunnels are located approximately 3.5 miles from the Hood River trailhead or only 1.1 miles from the Mosier side. While the whole trail offers marvelous scenery, people with limited time might want to start at the Mosier trailhead in order to access the Twin Tunnels and surrounding vistas more quickly.

On the Hood River side, the visitor center is located at MP 68.25. The first great viewpoint is near MP 70—where the curvy masonry walls overlook Inspiration Point and the syncline. The next viewpoint is around MP 71 at the wide spot marking the Wasco County line. One mile farther are the Twin Tunnels. MP 72 is actually in the east tunnel—across the tunnel from the '1921 snowbound' inscription. If you're curious about the inscription, ask in the visitor center to see the article about it.

The Twin Tunnels

Gorge Attraction/Mountain Views

34

Roundtrip time-guess from Portland: 2.5 hours
from Hood River: 30 minutes

Difficulty level: easy drive-up viewpoint
Highlights: The whole valley stretching to Mt. Hood

Panorama Point Park

Don't miss this nearby drive-to viewpoint of the picturesque Hood River Valley. This small park provides parking, restrooms and picnic tables so that you can relax and soak up the panoramic view from Mt. Hood to Mt. Adams.

Panorama Point is always a photographer's delight... springtime has Mt. Hood floating over a sea of white pear blossoms and all through the summer a riot of wildflowers surrounds the whole park. So Nice! This is a great place to quickly drive to from downtown when the clouds are setting up for an epic sunset. (If gate is closed, park and walk in.)

How about a sing-along! Try this refrain from 'America the Beautiful':

Oh beautiful for spacious skies,
For amber waves of grain,
For purple mountain majesties,
Above the fruited plain!

America! America!
God shed his grace on thee,
And crown thy good with brotherhood,
From sea to shining sea...

This captures the essence of the park perfectly!

Summertime explosion of California poppies

HEY: For Missoula flood slueths (like the author), note Van Horn Butte down in the valley—it's the small conical hill with orchards on it (looking at Hood, it's in the foreground at 11 o'clock). A boulder of white granite that rested atop the butte puzzled early 1900's geologists. The riddle as to how this granite got up there perplexed most scientists until the flood theory became gradually accepted in the mid-1900s. Geologists (except for those nutty creationists) now agree that the boulder arrived at this 850-feet-above sea level perch by floating here inside an iceberg that got stranded on this butte as the 1000-foot-high floodwaters receded. The boulder is Canadian granite…moved via glacier then flood to Hood River!

A purple-ish mountain over a fruited plain

A depth-of-field challenge

DRIVING: **From Hood River:** At the Hwy 35 4-way stop go south on Hwy 35 for 0.3 miles. Turn left onto Eastside Road. Follow this 1.5 miles, staying right at the junction, to the signed entrance on the right for Panorama Point County Park.

From Portland: Take I-84 to Hood River exit 64. Turn right and go uphill to the 4-way stop and follow above directions.

- Drivetime from Portland: 60 min
- from Hood River: 5 min
- Fee: free
- Restroom: yes

Waterfall/Swimming Hole

35

Roundtrip time-guess from Portland: 3.5 hours
from Hood River: 1.5 hours

Difficulty level: steep trail down to falls
Highlights: Diving, swimming, sunning

Punchbowl Falls

A popular sunbathing, cliff jumping, and hangout spot where the west fork of the Hood River plunges 10 feet into the 'Punchbowl'. It's worth going just to see the spectacular 75-foot columnar basalt walls rimming the huge aquamarine pool! On hot summer days you'll often see daredevils jumping from the basalt perches into the deep and chilly pool. Some people go

DRIVING: **From Hood River:** At the 13th and Oak stoplight turn up 13th St. Go through the Heights district and zigzag 3 times until you come to a stopsign (the road changes names to Tucker Road). Go left here at the Wind Master Market gas station (your last chance for snacks and drinks). Drive 8.0 miles, passing Tucker Park/camp, following the signs for Dee. Turn right at Dee (an old lumber mill) and cross the tracks and bridge. At the T-intersection go right onto Punchbowl Road and follow it, staying right, for 1.0 miles to a gravel pullout on the right side. (If you cross a bridge you've gone too far.)

From Portland: Take I-84 east to Hood River exit 62. Go right onto Cascade, follow it past Safeway until you get to a stoplight (13th and Oak). Turn right at light and follow above directions.

- **Drivetime from Portland: 72 min**
- **from Hood River: 17 min**
- **Fee: free**
- **Restroom: no**

over the falls on inner tubes and some just go body surfing! Join the fun or have a beer and watch the action from the scenic rim. From the rim you can also see pretty Dead Point Creek falling into its shaded grotto across the river.

Punchbowl is a Hood River classic...a cool, non-windy spot to hang out on a hot summer day.

EXPLORE: Head around the gate down the old road. In a few hundred yards there are a variety of spur trails that lead to different places along the rim. A super-steep staircase-like trail leads down to the falls and fish ladder. Past Punchbowl's rim the dirt road continues .25 miles to the river-level confluence of the east and west forks of the Hood.

The Fuller sisters—former Canadian Olympic stars

Lake/Mtn Views/Old-Growth

36

Roundtrip time-guess from Portland: 6 hours
from Hood River: 4 hours

Difficulty level: easy or difficult trails
Highlights: Postcard Mt. Hood view, boat rentals, fish, camp

Lost Lake

Lost Lake is amazing. It has something for everyone—beauty, serenity, old-growth…hiking, fishing, camping, swimming… day-use picnic tables, and a boat rental fleet.

This natural lake, northwest of Mt. Hood at 3,140 feet, is one of the most photographed lakes in the northwest and it has been a Hood River and Portland favorite for generations. Alas, sometimes it chokes on its own popularity; summer weekends can be a zoo! As many as 1,000 people may visit the lake on weekend

The view of Mt. Hood is mesmerizing

DRIVING: **From Hood River:** At the 13th and Oak stoplight turn up 13th St. Go through the Heights district and zigzag 3 times until you come to a stopsign (the road changes names to Tucker Road). Go left here at the Wind Master Market gas station (your last chance for snacks and drinks). Drive 8.0 miles, passing Tucker Park/camp, following the signs for Dee. Turn right at Dee (an old lumber mill) and cross the tracks and bridge. At the T-intersection turn left onto Lost Lake Road and follow it 13.5 winding miles to the lake's entrance booth.

- **Drivetime from Portland: 100 min**
- **from Hood River: 45 min**
- **Fee: $6 per car**
- **Restroom: yes**

From Portland: Take I-84 east to Hood River exit 62. Go right onto Cascade, follow it past Safeway until you get to a stoplight (13th and Oak). Turn right at light and follow above directions.

The old-growth walkway

days. If you go with this expectation you'll have a good time—it's fun to see so many happy people frolicking... throwing sticks for dogs, couples canoodling in canoes, sunbathers on rafts, family barbeques, etc.

If you want serenity and solitude you better plan to visit weekdays of after Labor Day. A Sept. stroll along the old-growth walkway then over to the western shore for an epic view of Mt. Hood framed by fall colors will make your heart sing (in July the song would be a chorus, in June/ Sept you could sing a solo)!

Hiking: There are three main hiking options. First, an easy 3.0 mile lakeshore trail is suitable and fun for everyone. Second is an old-growth walkway. This .75 mile handicap accessible raised wooden walkway travels through a gorgeous stand of old-growth fir, hemlock, and cedar on the north shore. The third and strenuous option is a hike to Lost Lake Butte. This trail, starting at the Campground B/C entrance, climbs 1,500 feet in 2.0 miles to the old lookout site atop the butte...spy Hood, Jefferson, and Adams from the top. Info about all the trails is available at the entrance booth and General Store.

Boating: Rent rowboats, canoes, and paddleboats by the hour or by the day. A large fleet is available, but the whole bunch usually rent out early on weekends. Bringing a canoe or kayak is a great idea.

Fishing: Fishing is a popular pastime at the lake because the fish are both big and dumb! Huge Rainbow trout are stocked yearly. The store has all the tips, equipment, bait, and licenses you need.

Camping: The huge campground has 137 sites. Tent and RV fees are $18-$25, and cabins are $50-$100 per night. Because this campground is wildly popular you have to be both savvy and prepared. First, there are no reservations—first come, first served. Second, Roy, the owner, says that in summer all the sites are usually full by early Friday, and some people come up as early as Wednesday to pitch a tent in a prime site for the weekend. The General Store has wood, ice, food, drinks, beer, etc., but being the only store within 20 miles qualifies it for airport-like pricing.

Picnicking: The picnic tables along the west shore are sweet. The view of Mt. Hood is epic and the kids can play and swim within sight. Get there early to have a prayer of obtaining one of the best sites.

Scenic Hike/Waterfall

37

Roundtrip time-guess from Portland: 5 hours
from Hood River: 2.75 hours

Difficulty level: moderate 2-mile one-way
Highlights: Creekside trail to big waterfall

Tamanawas Falls Trail

An idyllic deep-forest trail follows rushing Cold Spring Creek 2 miles up to spectacular Tamanawas Falls. This waterfall is a 125-foot daddy that pours steadily over a rocky escarpment into a mossy and rainbowed basin. This hike is a Hood River favorite—expect plenty of company on summer days. The trail climbs gradually, hugging the bank of beautiful Cold Spring Creek for much of its length. At the falls surefooted folk can scramble across a rocky slope to a large dry alcove behind the cascade—quite enchanting!

Because this trail has a well-deserved reputation for beauty and family-friendliness, it's tough to avoid crowds on windless summer days and weekends. If you want to bring your boyfriend in the hope of smooching in the romantic alcove…then maybe try to plan a hike in the early morning or near sunset.

For more solitude, try these lesser-known waterfall trails of similar length and beauty: Dry Creek Falls (entry 9), Falls Creek Falls (entry 15), or Elowah Falls (entry 5).

A bridge over untroubled water

DRIVING: **From Hood River:** At the Hwy 35 4-way stop sign, go south on Hwy 35, towards Mt. Hood, for 23.5 miles. The large gravel trailhead area is at MP 72.5, just before Sherwood campground.

From Portland: Take I-84 to Hood River exit 64. Turn right and go uphill to the 4-way stop and follow above directions.

- **Drivetime from Portland: 80 min**
- **from Hood River: 25 min**
- **Fee: NW Forest Pass (at Ranger station on Hwy 35)**
- **Restroom: no**

HIKE: From the parking area head right to the footbridge spanning the East Fork Hood River. Cross the bridge and go right on the trail signed Tamanawas Falls. After .5 miles stay left at the trail junction and then cross the Cold Spring Creek bridge. The trail stays near the creek for the next 1.0 miles then bonks into an avalanche area. Take the Elk Meadows trail upwards for 50 yards then stay left on a new primitive trail that picks its way across the avalanche zone. Now just .25 miles to the waterfall. Traverse the wet rocky slope to get to the alcove. Return the way you came.

An icy hike on Halloween '03

The name is tough to pronounce, but the sight may leave you speechless anyhow

Mosier Creek Falls/Pioneer Cemetery

Waterfall/Swimming Hole

38

Roundtrip time-guess from Portland: 3 hours
from Hood River: .75 hours or all day

Difficulty level: easyish path to see falls, but steep descent to pool

Highlights: Swimming hole and historic site

"In 1854 Jonah Mosier settled here so he could use this waterfall to power a sawmill", reads a trailside park bench overlooking Mosier Creek Falls. This cascading two-tiered 100-foot waterfall, just a short walk from downtown Mosier, is a popular local swimming hole and sunning spot. The reason is a nice deepish pool between the tiers that's fun to jump into from the surrounding rocks. The water is surprisingly warm in the summer (at

Whose turn to jump?

least by Gorge standards). Kids love it on ultra hot days—it's like a mini-Punchbowl falls! The waterfall and pool area also get great happy-hour sunshine, so if you go around 5pm on a hot summer day, expect some drinkin'!

Little Pocket Park on the northern bluff above the falls features a scattering of park benches, a pioneer cemetery, and some easy trails meandering the rim of Mosier Creek Gorge. Don't leave without checking out the fantastic syncline view (the serpentine basalt wall across the river) from the cemetery area.

Pioneer gravestone

Lower portion of Mosier Falls, as seen from the rim trail.

DRIVING: **From Hood River:** Take I-84 east to Mosier exit 69. Go right at the stop and into town. Drive through Mosier a few hundred yards and cross the bridge. The trail to the falls begins at a park bench on the far side of the bridge.

From Portland: Same as above.

- Drivetime from Portland: 65 min
- from Hood River: 9 min
- Fee: free
- Restroom: no

Scenic Hike/Wildflowers/Columbia Views

39

Roundtrip time-guess from Portland: 3.5 hours
from Hood River: 1.5 hours

Difficulty level: easy 1-mile one-way
Highlights: Wildflowers galore in April/May

Rowena Plateau Trail

Starting at the Rowena Crest viewpoint on the Historic Columbia River Highway, this 1-mile trail is an easy meandering stroll atop the fairly level plateau. On the trail's left is the Rowena Dell while on the right are the Columbia and the mouth of the Klickitat River. In the spring this trail is famous for its bonanza of wildflowers! Wildlife such as squirrels and raptors populate the swales around the two unique plateau lakes (the lakes were created when Missoula floodwaters raged up to 300 feet over this plateau top. The swirling currents of the floods carved out the two depressions that are now lakes as well as carving a huge portion of Rowena Dell).

The trail itself circles the first lake then continues to the very western end of the plateau where Memaloose Island, an ancient Indian burial site, rises in the middle of the Columbia. This is a really pleasant walk amidst beautiful eastern Gorge scenery.

The Nature Conservancy Trailhead

DRIVING: **From Hood River:** Take I-84 east to Mosier exit 69. Turn right and go through town, then 6 more miles to the Rowena Crest viewpoint. At the viewpoint entrance, park at the 4-car gravel pullout on the left where you see the Rowena Plateau sign. Or, head east on I-84 to Rowena exit 76. Turn right then right again, taking the Hist Hwy back west for 3 miles as it climbs to the Rowena Crest viewpoint.
From Portland: Same as above.

- **Drivetime from Portland: 73 min**
- **from Hood River: 18 min**
- **Fee: free**
- **Restroom: no**

Ahhh, the view past Lyle is a stunner!

HIKE: Start at the 5-step staircase going over the fence. Be sure to pick up the Nature Conservancy info brochure—if it's available. Make a donation in the box if you wish.

The trail begins towards the Dell. In .3 miles a spur trail goes off right around the first lake, to the cliff edge, then back to the main trail. The trail then continues .5 miles to the end of the plateau.

Balsamroot everywhere!

Scenic Hike/Columbia and Mountain Views

40

Roundtrip time-guess from Portland: 4.5 hours
from Hood River: 2.5 hours

Difficulty level: Moderate 1.5 miles one-way
Highlights: Wildflowers, Mt. Hood, Mt. Adams

McCall Point Trail

A wonderful slice of the eastern Gorge—possibly the best! This 1.5 mile trail climbs 1,000 feet to the McCall Point hilltop (named after Governor Tom McCall, 1967-1975). In April and May a riot of color along the whole trail makes this a favorite hike for wildflower chasers. The trail seems like one long viewpoint that becomes more magnificent the higher you hike. The first .5 miles are on an 1800's wagon trail through a wildflower meadow. Then, for the final 1.0 miles, the trail enters the oaken hills and steepens as it switchbacks to the top. What a great hilltop picnic area—views of Mt. Hood, Mt. Adams, and the Columbia from Hood River to Rowena!

The previous sign... R.I.P.

Looking west past swaying balsamroot

DRIVING: **From Hood River:** Take I-84 east to Mosier exit 69. Turn right and go through town, then 6 more miles to the Rowena Crest viewpoint. Turn right and park where the masonry wall begins. **Or,** head east on I-84 to Rowena exit 76. Turn right then right again, taking the Hist Hwy back west for 3 miles as it climbs to the Rowena Crest viewpoint.
From Portland: Same as above.

- **Drivetime from Portland: 73 min**
- **from Hood River: 18 min**
- **Fee: free**
- **Restroom: no**

Looking down on Rowena Dell and Mt. Adams

HIKE: The trail starts at the south side of the Rowena Crest viewpoint parking area. After .5 miles turn right at the Nature Conservancy sign. There are short spur trails to vista points but the main trail is easy to follow to the top. At the hilltop a trail leads down onto private property, but this spacious hilltop is this hike's end. Return the way you came.

Gorge Attraction/Columbia and Mountain Views

41

Roundtrip time-guess from Portland: 3.5 hours
from Hood River: 1.25 hours

Difficulty level: easy drive-up viewpoint
Highlights: Wow!

Courtney Road Viewpoint

Incredibly stunning and adjective defying—this vista is the definition of **Gorge-ous!** Unquestionably this is the best drive-to viewpoint in the mid-Columbia region...and it's not even hard to get to. From Hwy 14 it's just a 15-minute, 4-mile winding drive.

From this 1,600-foot perch the Columbia sweeps east past Memaloose Island and Rowena Plateau on its way to The Dalles. Mt. Hood towers at the head of the Hood River Valley while the Mosier Twin Tunnels and Chicken Charlie Island are below. (The island has a neat history: in 1903 a man moved his chicken farm to the island because he was being eaten out of business by coyotes and raccoons on the mainland. Later, near 1920, Charlie Reither "claimed" the island, and began growing hay on his bigger pre-dam land. Amazingly he built a narrow-gauge railroad, on which he ran a Model-T Ford as the engine, in order to harvest the hay.)

To the west 4,950-foot Mt. Defiance frames the Columbia with 2,948-foot Dog Mountain. Notice that on this viewpoint you're actually straddling the divide between the 'wet-side' and the 'dry-side' of the Gorge. Watching a summer sunset here is Magnifico!

Poetry to the west

Stunning to the east

DRIVING: **From Hood River:** Cross HR bridge and go right on Hwy 14 for 4.5 miles. Pass MP 69 and turn left onto Courtney road and begin a steep ascent. The first 2.1 miles are paved, but when the road turns to dirt stay with it for .6 miles until the road forks. Left goes to a B'n'B. You want the right fork, marked on a small sign 'H5000' that leads behind the B'n'B. Follow this 1.3 miles until…WOW, panorama-rama! Around the bend there's a new house on the left, so park on the right by the boulders and walk up the hill. **From Portland:** Take I-84 to Hood River exit 64 then follow above directions.

Majestic to the south

Exploration/Scenic Hike

42

Roundtrip time-guess from Portland: 4 hours
from Hood River: 1.75 hours

Difficulty level: moderate .5 miles one-way
Highlights: Mysterious walls and pits

Indian Vision Quest Pits Trail

A short but moderately uphill 0.5 mile jaunt leads to a surprising and fascinating ancient Indian site. Strange pits, walls, and rock piles cover a vast rocky slope. Historians suggest that these 'Indian Pits' were erected by Indian youths as a rite-of-passage. The adolescents would spend nights up here toiling, fasting, and sleep-deprived in an effort to bring forth spirit visions to guide them in their adult lives. Numerous examples of these pits exist throughout the Gorge and there's a signboard explaining the history atop Wind Mtn. (entry 17). Perhaps this site was revered because it overlooks two significant landmarks: Memaloose Island (the Indian Isle of the Dead) and Wy'east (Mt. Hood). The sense of history is palpable in this meditative place. Imagine the Columbia in 1805—what would an Indian think about Lewis and Clark venturing downstream?

A pits-eye view east along the Columbia

DRIVING: **From Hood River:** Cross HR bridge and go right on Hwy 14 for 5.7 miles. Pass MP 70 and just before MP 71, turn left onto Old Hwy No. 8. Follow this 1 mile around the lake and up. **Careful**—look for a one-car spot on the left side of the road next to a red mailbox. There is a gate with a 'Road Closed' sign. Park there.

From Portland: Take I-84 to Hood River exit 64 then follow above directions.

- **Drivetime from Portland: 70 min**
- **from Hood River: 15 min**
- **Fee: free**
- **Restroom: no**

EXPLORE: Around the gate begin hiking up the obvious trail. After about .3 miles uphill you reach the edge of a ridge where you can gaze left to the rocky slope and look for the zigzagging walls. The trail continues down from here to the slope level, making a sharp turn to the left. From here you can continue about .75 miles more, winding through some pits until you come out to a grassy slope. The trail eventually fades, so it's best to turn back from here. Return the way you came in and please be respectful not to disturb this unregulated site.

A long wall zigzags amongst the pits

Catherine Creek Falls Stroll

Scenic Hike/Wildflowers/Columbia Views

43

Roundtrip time-guess from Portland: 3 hours
from Hood River: 1 hour

Difficulty level: easy 1-mile loop
Highlights: Wildflowers and Columbia views

Ahhhh...Catherine Creek...**once a junkyard, now a sanctuary. Wildflower heaven in the springtime.**

A paved 1.0 mile "wheelchair accessible" path meanders the gentle grassy hillsides above the Columbia. The eastern viewpoint showcases the creek tumbling over a 12-foot ledge into a little pool. A bench here has an inspired placement...ponder the stunning geology and the curvaceous river while accompanied by the waterfall's gurgle and music of the birds and bees... mmmmm. Adventurers can scramble down to the waterfall and check out the peculiar micro-gorge the creek has cut through the basalt.

This park is great for families—***your parents will love it***...as will anyone seeking mello terrain with stunning views! Springtime is best—the famed wildflowers spangle the hills and canyons and the creek flows happily (sadly, it dries up by July). Late afternoon sunlight is beautiful here—just like on the cover of this guide.

Looking east from the paved pathway

DRIVING: **From Hood River:** Cross HR bridge and go right on Hwy 14 for 5.7 miles. Pass MP 70 and just before MP 71, turn left onto Old Hwy No. 8. Proceed 1.5 miles around the lake, up to the plateau, and then pull off at the large Catherine Creek sign.

From Portland: Take I-84 to Hood River exit 64 then follow above directions.

Karen and Timber at the east viewpoint bench

HIKE: Cross the street from the parking area and read the signboard describing the paved pathway's options. The waterfall is just below the east viewpoint bench. The longest loop is best!

A black & white photo doesn't do justice to this June wildflower dazzle!

Scenic Hike/Exploration/Columbia Views

44

Roundtrip time-guess from Portland: 3.5 hours
from Hood River: 1.5 hours

Difficulty level: moderate 1.5-mile loop
Highlights: Hike through a giant rock arch

Catherine Creek Arch Trail

Such a unique hike—where else but the Gorge! Overall this scenic 1.5 mile trail is fairly easy, except for a 200-foot, loose-rock scramble. You get to climb up to the magnificent basalt arch and then squeeze through a narrow secret passageway to the top. Being under the arch itself is some Gorge magic—look up and try to make the sun peek around the edge like a diamond ring. Although the route may look sketchy, it's fun and unique with a killer view at the top.

The footpath then zigzags over easy terrain of grass and wildflowers, looping you back around to the arch's base.

The Arch

DRIVING: **From Hood River:** Cross HR bridge and go right on Hwy 14 for 5.7 miles. Pass MP 70 and just before MP 71, turn left onto Old Hwy No 8. Proceed 1.5 miles around the lake, up to the plateau, and then pull off at the large Catherine Creek sign.

From Portland: Take I-84 to Hood River exit 64 then follow above directions.

HIKE: From the parking area, go through the green gate then right on the faint roadbed marked "#21". In 100 yards, as the road becomes more defined, follow it about .3 miles, hop Catherine Creek, and stop at the old corral. From this corral look up to spot the arch. Less agile people should stop here and turn around.

To hike through the arch and complete the loop, follow the path that starts opposite the corral and leads through the trees to the rocky slope under the arch. Begin the 200-foot scramble over the decaying tree then up the rocks underneath the arch. Now, squeeze into the narrow path between the wall and the arch. Once up, go right to explore along the top of the arch—just because you can! Then, to finish the loop find the faint footpath that heads uphill. It soon bends to the right towards the powerlines. When you get to these powerlines go down and left to the junction with the dirt road. Go left and wind downhill back to the corral where you retrace your steps to your car.

The barn in 2002

The barn in 2005

Klickitat River Gorge Salmon Spawning

Gorge Attraction/Scenic Hike

45

Roundtrip time-guess from Portland: 4 hours
from Hood River: 1.5 hours

Difficulty level: easy .5-mile one-way
Highlights: Waterfall-leaping salmon!

Watch huge Chinook and Coho salmon jump a 7-foot waterfall on their once-in-a-lifetime spawning journey! The Klickitat River roars through a narrow basalt canyon upriver from its confluence with the Columbia. At the head of this canyon are the waterfall and fish ladder. Every autumn a new group of salmon impressively hurl themselves up these falls—some make it the hard way, some find the easier fish ladder. Quite a show!

These narrows are also an Indian dip-netting site. During the heart of the fall run you can respectfully sit and watch the traditional methods of catching the migrating salmon. On Sundays and Mondays no fishing is allowed and you see the most fish jumping. Go the other days if you'd prefer to see the netting techniques.

Typically the run lasts through Sept. and Oct. In

Hooray, Go Big!

DRIVING: **From Hood River:** Cross HR bridge and go right on Hwy 14 for 10.6 miles. Just past the Klickitat bridge, before Lyle, turn left on Route 142. Go 1.5 miles then turn left onto Fisher Bridge road. Just over the bridge park on the wide dirt area where the road turns right.

From Portland: Take I-84 to Hood River exit 64 then follow above directions.

- **Drivetime from Portland: 74 min**
- **from Hood River: 17 min**
- **Fee: free**
- **Restroom: no**

big years like 2001-2004 the fish jumped like popcorn—maybe 10-30 per minute! In low years or on days when the fish are "spooked" (by some unknown river situation) you may not see any fish jumping. Bring a beer in case the fish are poppin', cuz it's a hoot to sit and cheer their tenacity against the unrelenting falls!

HIKE: From the parking area climb up to the old railroad bed. Start upriver on the gravel trail around the gate. It's about a .5 mile stroll to the falls. Go right when you meet the dirt road and follow it upstream then down to the fish ladder (look for the large metal pipe).

Indians dip-netting

Scenic Hike/Columbia Views

46

Roundtrip time-guess from Portland: 4.5 hours
from Hood River: 2 hours

Difficulty level: mod/diff 2 miles one-way
Highlights: Peaceful grassy bluffs

Cherry Orchard Trail

A steep trail leads up to the bluffs east of Lyle, then continues up to and along the top of the ridge. The trail is on private property, but the owner graciously invites the public to enjoy this beautiful slice of land. The whole trail, from river to ridgetop, is a mod/diff 2 miles. The steepest part is first—the 10 minutes it takes to climb to the plateau...but wow, the cliffs, the river views, and the dramatic geology are worth the huffing and puffing! These flat grassy plateaus are a great place to picnic, watch Rowena windsurfers, or catch a summer sunset with a lover and a bottle of wine. These bluffs, just like Rowena Plateau across the river, were scoured by many 1000-foot walls of floodwater during the repetitive Ice-age floods that raged through the Gorge.

Past the plateau the trail continues steeply on up to the ridge. The views get better the whole way, but lots of folks just stop at the plateaus to meander around. For those that continue, the trail ascends to the ridge, flattens out, and traipses east across the hillside for another mile before dead-ending at the clearing where the old-time cherry orchard grew. Explore around a little...enjoy the uncommon eastern Gorge views... maybe you'll stumble onto one of the abandoned cherry trees just bursting with pickable delights!

Sign-in box

DRIVING: **From Hood River:** Cross HR bridge and go right on Hwy 14 for 12 miles. Pass Lyle and go through two tunnels. Just past the second tunnel look for the large pullout on the left and park there.

From Portland: Take I-84 to Hood River exit 64 then follow above directions.

- **Drivetime from Portland: 75 min**
- **from Hood River: 17 min**
- **Fee: free**
- **Restroom: no**

Looking over the bluffs towards The Dalles

HIKE: From the center of the parking area find the path that goes up and over the fence. Hike a few hundred yards until you get to the signpost and waiver box. Sign-in, then climb about .3 miles (10 minutes) watching for the plateau spur. This spur trail goes left from the main trail, quickly passes some poison oak shrubs, then meanders west across the plateaus. Explore anywhere your heart desires.

If you keep going past the plateau, the trail switchbacks upwards for .75 miles. Reaching the top the trail levels and begins a pleasant 1.0-mile ramble through an oak and pine forest. The trail ends where it intersects with a dirt road. Go right on the road to explore the cleared orchard site and some views. Head back the way you came.

Sweet western view from the top of the trail

Horsethief Butte/Columbia Hills S.P. Petroglyphs

Gorge Attraction/Petroglyphs/Columbia & Mtn Views

47

Roundtrip time-guess from Portland: 5 hours
from Hood River: 2.5 hours

Difficulty level: easy petroglyph view, moderate trails
Highlights: Epic petroglyphs, fun-to-explore outcropping

Sherry and Tom bouldering

Horsethief Butte is a fortress-like 100-foot-high outcropping of basalt perched above the Columbia. This popular horseshoe-shaped butte has a variety of trails that lead up to, around, and into it. Once inside, the fun-to-explore paths crisscross around and over a labyrinth of walls. On weekends there are usually rock-climbing schools teaching skills on the walls as well as plenty of 'boulderers' scaling their 'problems'.

Curious people can scout for faded pictographs and petroglyphs adorning the rock walls both inside and outside the butte. The best ones are hard to find—there is no map, just explore with sharp eyes.

The views from atop the butte are sweeping. To the east note the rail bridge—Celilo Falls was located just beyond the bridge, before being flooded over by The Dalles dam. To the south Mt. Hood towers proudly over The Dalles.

If it's drizzling or gray around Hood River, head to Horsethief—chances are that it's dry!

The horseshoe entrance to the Bluff

DRIVING: **From Hood River:** Cross HR bridge and go right on Hwy 14 for 20 miles. Columbia Hills State Park is at MP 85, and the Butte is 1.5 miles past at MP 86.5. (Park on the hwy shoulder by the sign). **From Portland:** Take I-84 to Hood River exit 64 then follow above directions.

Tsagaglalal watches a Saturday tour group

NOTE: Newly-formed Columbia Hills State Park (formerly Horsethief), is now home to a treasure of petroglyphs. These glyphs were removed from their natural setting along the Columbia in the mid-1950's, before being inundated by the backwaters of the Dalles dam. For the last 50 years these glyphs have been stored at the dam, but in 2003 they were moved back to this park. Wow, these glyphs are classic... Spedis owls, water demons, and many more!

Spedis Owl

Also, the famed petroglyph Tsagaglalal, "she who watches", is nearby... but you can only see her on ranger-guided tours held on summer Fridays and Saturdays. Call 509-767-1159, weeks in advance, to reserve a space on these popular tours.

The new (2003) petroglyph-viewing walkway

Museum

48

Roundtrip time-guess from Portland: 5.5 hours
from Hood River: 3 hours

Difficulty level: easy
Highlights: Fun museum—learn everything!

Columbia Gorge Discovery Center

To anyone who has traveled the USA it's obvious that the Columbia River Gorge is a national treasure—one of nature's finest masterpieces! With so many visual splendors awaiting at every turn in the road...who can be blamed for feeling rushed to take it all in? Hurry Hurry Hurry!

But wait...slow down for a couple of hours and make sure to visit the Columbia Gorge Discovery Center.

<u>Do not miss this!</u>

The building, combining both the Discovery Center and the Wasco County Historical Museum, is both a visual and intellectual treat. Huge pictorial displays abound...Giant movie screens

The gorgeous atrium beckons you inside

DRIVING: **From Hood River:** Take I-84 east to Rowena exit 76. Go straight then right. At the stop sign turn left onto the Hist Hwy. Drive 4.3 miles and turn left onto Discovery Center road. **Or**, from The Dalles take I-84 exit 82 and go west 1.4 miles to Discovery Center road.

From Portland: Same as above.

- **Drivetime from Portland: 75 min**
- **from Hood River: 20 min**
- **Fee: Adults $6.50, less for kids & seniors**
- **Open year-round 9am-5pm**
- **Restroom: yes**

The Scenic Hwy in the 1920s

loop through fascinating videos… Actual cars, canoes, steam engines… And More. There's not much walking nor reading required in this museum—just settle on one of the many viewing benches and let the movies dazzle you with <u>Awesome Gorge Perspective:</u> *rumble, rumble,* the cataclysm theater fantastically explains the Gorge's formative slow flood of basalt followed by… *whooosh,* Ice-Age floods of water carve the "gorge" we see today…*beep, beep,* travel the Scenic Hwy via charismatic 1916 and 1931 movies…*toot, toot,* railroads race feverishly to build upstream along the Deschutes to get to Bend's timber…*slap, slap,* salmon jump as Indians net at Celilo Falls…*boom, boom,* dynamite blasts the construction of Bonneville and Dalles dams…*chant, chant,* red-robed Rajneeshees cheer the Bhagwan as he drives his Rolls Royce through the commune—way, way too much to learn—so, so fun!

Whew, now take a break in the Basalt Rock Café. It's got a full menu of sandwiches, burgers, soups, etc. at **great prices**—no need to leave to get lunch elsewhere.

<u>Plan for at least 2 hours here.</u> Maybe start with the main feature in the atrium (Lewis and Clark for '05 and '06) then check out the Gorge displays. After a refreshing bite, head into the Wasco side, watch the two brilliant videos inside the door…and then linger wherever your curiosity pulls. And, before you leave, wander outside into The Dalles sunshine and either tour the re-created 1848 exhibits or take your dog for a walk down the 1.5-mile path that meanders towards the Columbia.

Wake up, get coffee, get breakfast, and get there for the 9am opening. Bring the kids—they love all the hands-on displays, play 'n' learn areas, and discovery doors placed low where they can peek at them. **You will enjoy exploring the Gorge much more after a couple hours here!**

Waterfall/Exploration/Swimming Hole

49

Roundtrip time-guess from Portland: 7 hours
from Hood River: 4 hours

Difficulty level: easyish (but long) staircase descent
Highlights: Majestic desert waterfall, killer swimming holes

White River Falls State Park

This dramatic two-tiered 137-foot waterfall is surprisingly located 30 miles south of The Dalles amidst the hot dry grasslands of the Tygh Valley. Great for a full-day getaway—plan a trip here on one of those windless too-hot gorge days. You'll love a day of swimming, exploring, photography, and relaxation.

The White River originates on Mt. Hood and flows east through the hot Tygh Valley where it slows down and warms up. Just before its confluence with the Deschutes River it tumbles over a series of basalt ledges that make up White River Falls. The first drop is a rainbow-spawning 90-foot beauty. The river then pools to plunge another 45 feet into a rounded basin—the two falls, seen together, are very camera friendly (photos are best in the morning).

Staircase, trail, beach, and power plant

A short steep staircase-like trail leads down from the viewing area. You'll need to go down this trail a bit for the epic falls view. At the trail's bottom is an abandoned 1901 power plant building. Farther downstream the trail leads to a third waterfall and plenty of flat ledges and small beaches for sunning, swimming, and picnicking—explore to find your own skinnydipping spot!

DRIVING: **From Hood River:** Take I-84 east to The Dalles exit 87. Turn right and cross the railroad bridge to a stop sign. Turn left onto Hwy 197 towards Dufur and Bend. Follow Hwy 197 for 28 miles south. Just past MP 33, at a blinking light, turn left onto Hwy 216 and go 4 miles to the park.

From Portland: Same as above.

- **Drivetime from Portland: 2 hours**
- **from Hood River: 1 hour**
- **Fee: free**
- **Restroom: yes**

NOTE: Since you've come this far, leave time for a super-scenic 30-minute bonus drive as you head home. From the park head east 3 miles down to Sherars Falls on the Deschutes River. Cross the bridge and turn right onto River Road…it follows the river's curves for 8 miles to Maupin—Gorgeous! In Maupin restock the cooler with some "roadies", get back on Hwy 197, and floor-it back to The Dalles!

Skinny-dipper's heaven downstream

The epic view just a short jaunt down the trail

ICONIC GORGE ATTRACTIONS

Here is a list of some of the Gorge's other attractions that aren't featured in this guide, which may be of interest to both visitors and locals.

Historic Lodges/ Restaurants

Columbia Gorge Hotel: Hood River, OR 541-386-5566
www.columbiagorgehotel.com

Beautiful romantic and historic hotel on a bluff above the Columbia. Great river view, exquisite gardens, waterfall.

Timberline Lodge: Gov't Camp/Mt Hood, OR 503-622-7979
www.timberlinelodge.com

Classic 1930's lodge/restaurant at the base of Timberline ski resort. Glorious Mt Hood views!

Multnomah Falls Lodge: at the Falls, I-84 exit 31, OR 503-695-2376
www.multnomahfallslodge.com

Charming restaurant/ lounge at the base of the Falls. Gift shop and National Forest info center.

The Lyle Hotel: Lyle, WA 509-365-5953
www.lylehotel.com

Small and intimate hotel/restaurant in the quaint town of Lyle. Near Klickitat river and gateway to eastern gorge wineries.

Golf, Food, & Drinks

Skamania Lodge: Stevenson, WA 509-427-7700
www.skamania.com

Large modern lodge/golf course/restaurant/conference center sporting great views from a spacious patio.

McMenamins Edgefield: Troutdale, OR 503-669-8610
www.mcmenamins.com

Funky large hotel/hostel complex—micro-brewery, distillery, winery, par-3 golf course, restaurants and bars galore! FUN! FUN! FUN!

Indian Creek golf course: Hood River, OR 541-386-7770
www.indiancreekgolf.com

Fantastic course with picturesque views of both Mt Hood and Mt Adams. Top-notch bar/restaurant.

Hot Spring Resorts

Bonneville Hot Spring Resort: North Bonneville, WA 509-427-7767
www.bonnevilleresort.com

Large and new-ish resort/ spa/ restaurant/ conference center. Pools available to visitors.

Carson Hot Spring Resort: Carson, WA 509-427-8292

Rustic and historic European-type resort. Spa treatments, soaking tubs, etc. Walk-ins welcome.

Columbia River Tour Boats

Sternwheeler "Columbia Gorge": Cascade Locks, OR 541-374-8427
www.sternwheeler.com

Marvelous old-time river tour boat/ restaurant. Epic and unforgettable sightseeing cruises.

Queen of the West: Portland, OR 1-800-434-1232
www.americanweststeamboat.com
Multi-day cruises up the Columbia from Portland.

Railroad tours

Mt. Hood Scenic Railroad: Hood River, OR 541-386-3556
www.mthoodrr.com
Charming old-time rail tour of magnificent Hood River valley. Lunch, dinner, or sightseeing.

Museums

Maryhill Museum & Stonehenge mnmt: Goldendale, WA 509-773-3733
www.maryhillmuseum.org
Popular museum with international appeal. Gorgeous building and views. Nearby is Stonehenge life-size re-creation.

International Museum of Carousel Art: Hood River, OR 541-387-4622
www.carouselmuseum.com
Riveting collection of all things Carousel.

Whitewater Rafting

Wet Planet Rafting Inc., White Salmon, WA 509-493-8989
www.wetplanetwhitewater.com

Zoller's Outdoor Odysseys, White Salmon, WA 509-493-2641
www.zooraft.com

River Rider.com, Hood River, OR 541-386-7238
www.riverrider.com

All Adventures Rafting, White Salmon, WA 1-800-743-5628
www.alladventuresrafting.com

Fruit, Orchards, and Harvest (Map on page118)

Hood River Valley Fruit Loop 541-386-7697
www.hoodriverfruitloop.com
Epic 45-mile driving tour route through scenic valley. Orchards, fruitstands, wineries, quirky farms!

Wine Tasting (Map on page 119)

Columbia Gorge Winegrowers assoc. 1-866-413-wine
www.columbiagorgewine.com
A world of wine in 40 miles! Plan a tour of dozens of wineries in the Gorge's increasingly-acclaimed growing regions.

Micro-breweries

Big Horse Brew Pub: 115 State Hood River, OR 541-386-4411

Full Sail Brewing Co.: 506 Columbia Hood River, OR 541-386-2247

Elliot Glacier Public House: 4945 Baseline Parkdale, OR 541-352-4022

Liberator Brewery:20101 NE Sandy Blvd Troutdale,OR 503-665-2771

McMenamins Edgefield Brewery: 2126 SW Halsey Troutdale, OR 503-669-8610

Walking Man Brewing Co.: 240 SW First Stevenson, WA 509-427-5520

The gorgeous driving tour of Hood River Valley

This map, in a much larger, informative, and colorful form, is available for **free** throughout the Gorge.

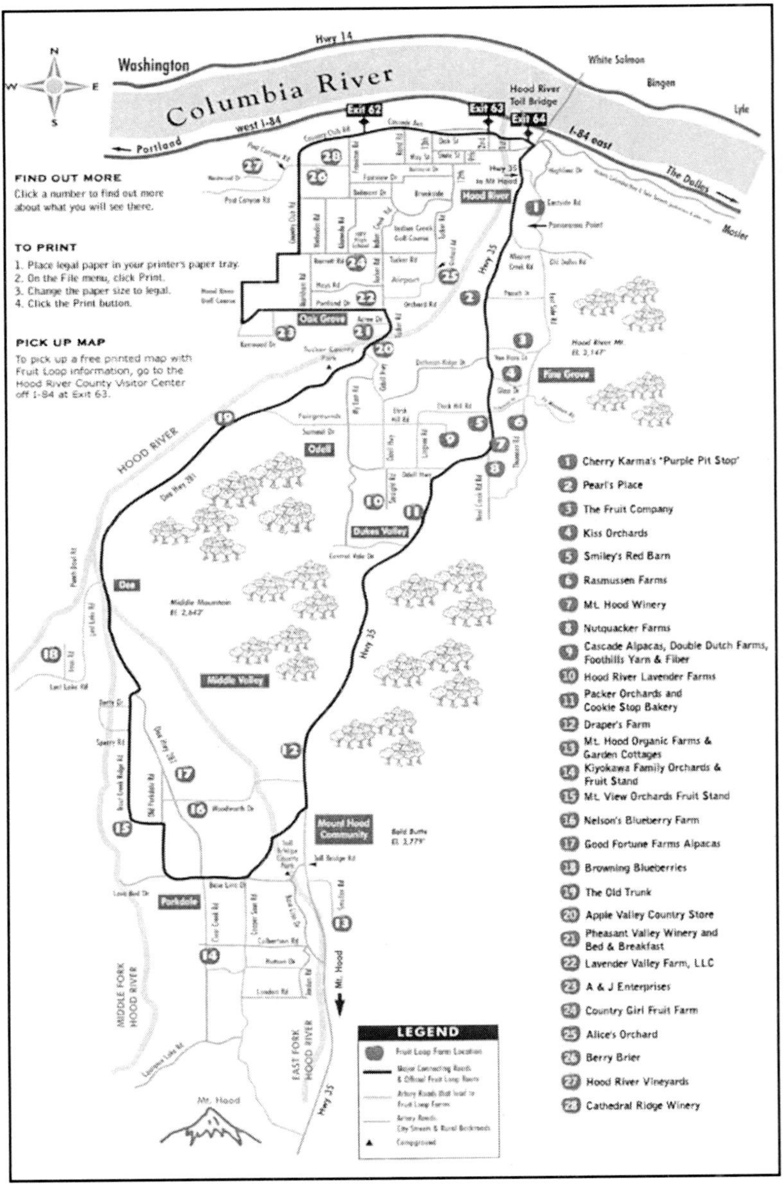

WINERIES MAP: The Gorge's newest tour route

This map, in its colorful glory with driving directions on the back, is available for **free** in the winegrower region.

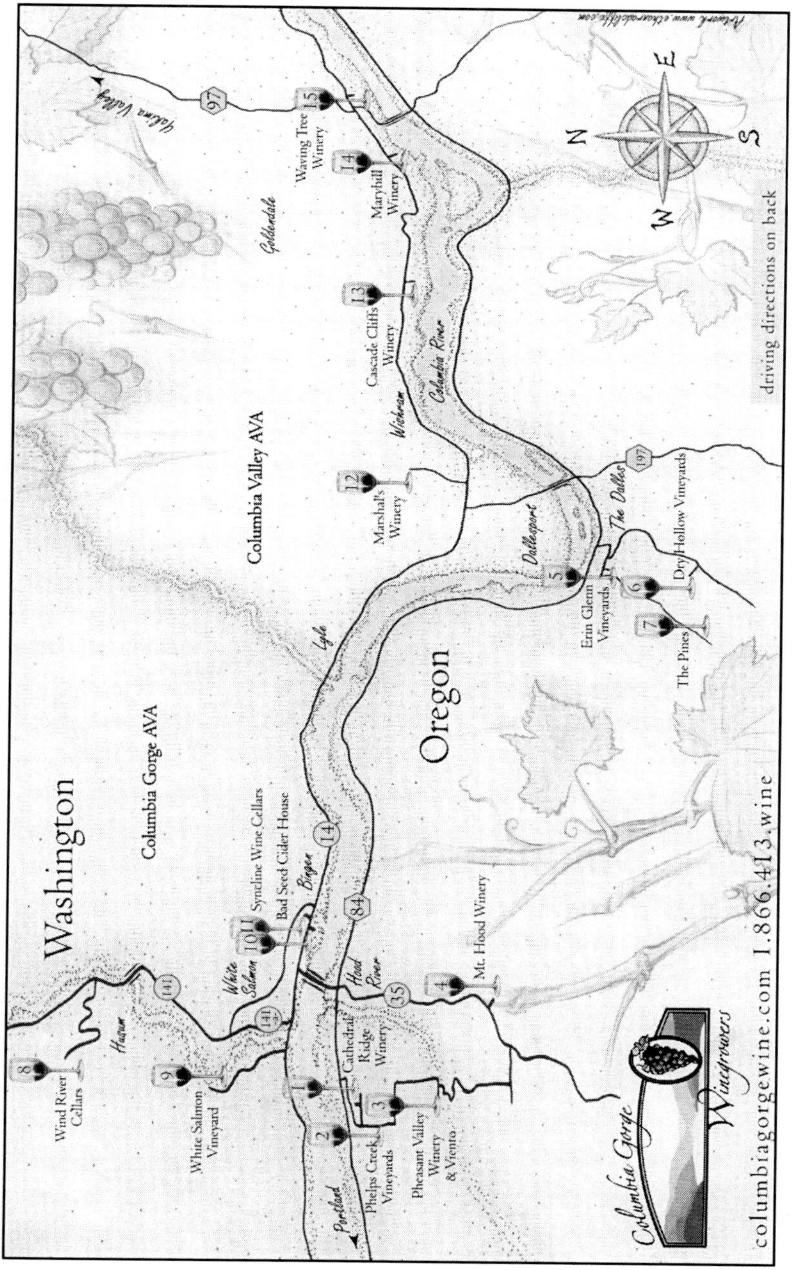

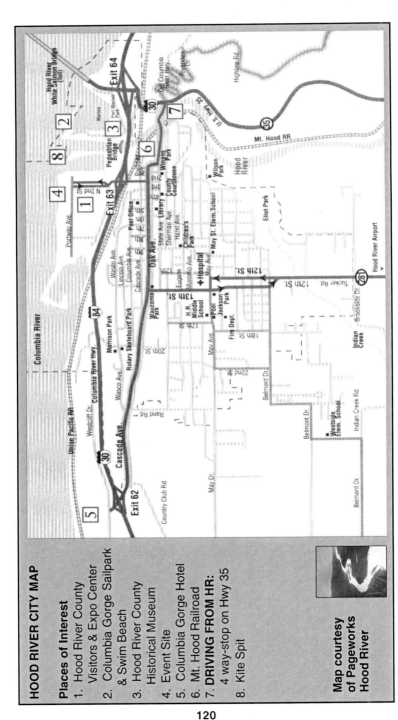

HOOD RIVER CITY MAP

Places of Interest

1. Hood River County Visitors & Expo Center
2. Columbia Gorge Sailpark & Swim Beach
3. Hood River County Historical Museum
4. Event Site
5. Columbia Gorge Hotel
6. Mt. Hood Railroad
7. **DRIVING FROM HR:** 4 way-stop on Hwy 35
8. Kite Spit

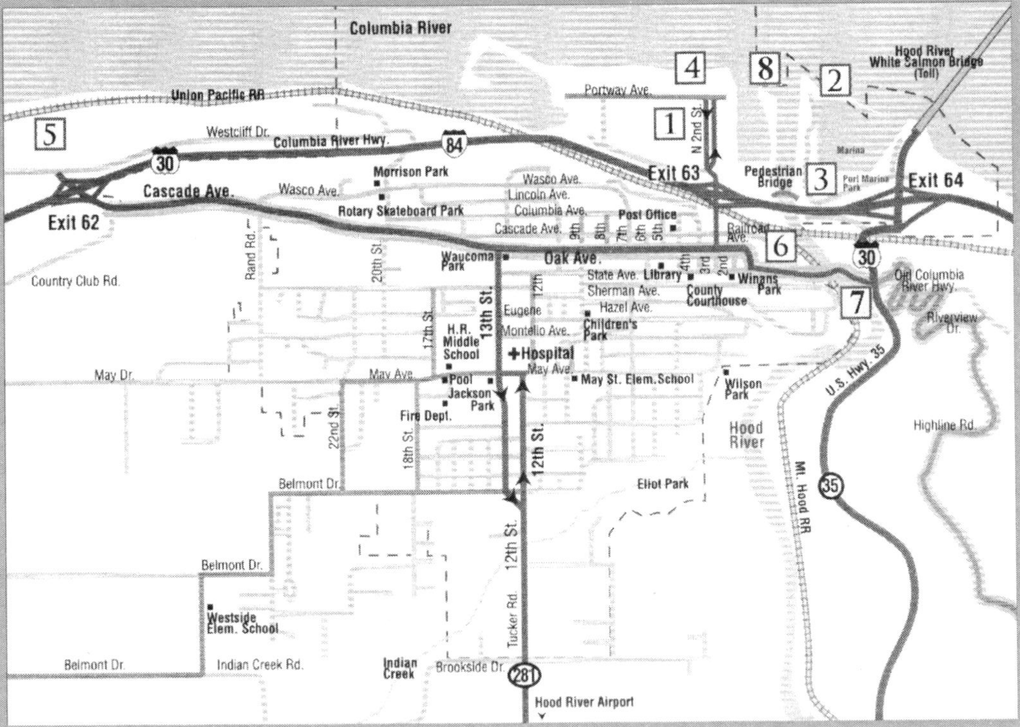

Map courtesy of Pageworks Hood River

If you've liked Curious Gorge...

for its variety, friendly tone, off-the-beaten-path ideas,
humor, and photo-riffic entries...
then you should see Scott's new Gorge guidebook

This is the guidebook where Scott really lets it all hang out!

"Pokin' Round" is a sexy, uninhibited R-rated guide to the Gorge's hidden treasures – a guide with a romantic and unabashedly naked twist. Get Excited – Scott invites you to bring your sweetie and to go explore the Gorge's nooks and crannies with a blanket and a bottle of wine in hand. Hoooo...Fun!

If you thought ***Curious Gorge*** was entertaining...then you ain't seen nothin' yet! Cookie knows the Gorge like few others. If you want an insider's look at a bunch of his favorite places, then find a copy of ***Pokin' Round the Gorge*** at one of the Gorge's FEARLESS retailers...or go to www.PokinRound.com to see the fun website, preview the book, and watch the funny behind-the-scenes videos.